Race Manners

RACE
MANNERS

NAVIGATING THE MINEFIELD BETWEEN BLACK AND WHITE AMERICANS

BRUCE A. JACOBS

Arcade Publishing • New York

FIRST EDITION

Their Eyes Were Watching God *by Zora Neale Hurston, copyright © 1937 by Harper & Row, Publishers, Inc. Renewed 1965 by John C. Hurston and Joel Hurston. Used by permission of HarperCollins Publishers, Inc.*

"Funny Vibe" by Vernon Reid, copyright © 1988 by Famous Music Corporation and Dare To Dream Music.

Library of Congress Cataloging-in-Publication Data

Jacobs, Bruce A.
    Race manners : navigating the minefield between Black and White Americans / Bruce A. Jacobs. —1st ed.
        p.   cm.
    ISBN 1-55970-453-5
    1. United States—Race relations. 2. Afro-Americans—Life skills guides. 3. Whites—United States—Life skills guides. I.Title.
E185.615.J297   1999
305.8'00973—dc21   98-49948

Published in the United States by Arcade Publishing, Inc., New York

Distributed by Little, Brown and Company

10 9 8 7 6 5 4 3 2 1

PRINTED IN THE UNITED STATES OF AMERICA

For my mother and father

The relation subsisting between the white and colored peoples of this country is the great, paramount, imperative, and all-commanding question for this age and nation to solve.
—Frederick Douglass

So why you want to give me that funny vibe?
—Living Colour

Contents

Acknowledgments

Race Manners has evolved in ways I could never have predicted. At times, I fought this book. As a poet and writer, I dreaded the thought of writing about personal issues of race, even as I abhorred the mess we have made of public dialogue. Sometimes the very idea of this book seemed impossible. I walked away from the project more than once. But I always found myself drawn back to it again. What made it so forbidding was also what made it worth attempting. I had to know if I could pull it off.

Without the help of others, I might have struggled forever. I thank my editor, Tim Bent, who saw in my first manuscript things I would not come to see until later, and my agent, Sheree Bykofsky, whose faith and dedication (not to mention stamina) know no bounds. This was a labor of love for them as well. My thanks to Chateau de Lesvault, to Ucross Foundation, and to MacDowell Colony, where I conceived this book in fits and starts amid other work. And to Mary and the guys, who nourished and counseled me through even the worst of times, and to Ruth, Barrett, Ken, my family, and the other people in my life whose love and wisdom have sustained and inspired me, I will always be grateful.

Woods Hole, Massachusetts
June 1998

Race Manners

Introduction

Fear of Frankness

Our country is consuming itself in racial rage. Increasingly, talk about race carries either the tone of violence or a sense of sterile, exaggerated civility. The message seems to be, Shut up and behave before somebody gets hurt. Talking about race is, quite literally, dangerous.

My older sister, a public health educator, told me a story recently about having attended a "cultural diversity" seminar of the kind that by now has become an American staple. When the agenda came to the subject of African Americans, a black female facilitator rose to her feet. The woman proceeded to give a crisp lecture to the large, multiethnic audience on the values and characteristics of African Americans: how they speak, how they like to be treated, how they interact with others. She spared no detail, taking care to explain, for instance, that African Americans tend to avoid direct eye contact because they consider such forwardness disrespectful. She exuded authority, presenting the nature of black people as one might the rules of spelling.

As the facilitator confidently reeled off these cultural attributes, my sister felt a sinking realization: not one of these "facts" about black people was true of her, or of those close to her. She raised her hand and voiced her dissent. A polite argument with the facilitator ensued. My sister asked how anyone could arrive at such cut-and-dried conclusions about blacks. The facilitator replied rather curtly that, in her experience, she had found certain general tendencies to be true. My sister said just as curtly that, as an African American, she found none of these "tendencies" to be accurate in any general way. The conversation continued, with the facilitator finally yielding the point that experience is relative. My sister emerged feeling both vindicated and dismayed.

It's not that my sister or I disapprove of diversity seminars: she herself is a facilitator who runs conflict-resolution and cultural diversity workshops. Both she and I feel strongly about the need to help people confront their own biases and respect others' cultures. Nor are we naive about the massive problem of bigotry in corporate and institutional America (the recent multimillion-dollar discrimination settlement involving Texaco employees is just one prominent example). But we both shook our heads in amazement at a racial climate so desperate that even the shallowest of approaches can be rushed into the void with formulaic "answers" — and be taken seriously.

How did things become this insane? What has possessed us to delegate our powers of cultural perception, in the worst case, to glib consultants spouting generalizations? And why, forty years after White Only and Colored Only signs on water fountains, are we too often willing to accept versions of one another's identities that are as contrived and as facile as car ads?

The reason is that race has become so toxic a topic in America that many of us are afraid to even touch it, at least in public, without some kind of industrial-strength protection. With talk-show vitriol now passing for social discourse, and with racial anger mounting in proportion to the fears and insecurities of a downsized America, the topic of race has acquired the potency of nerve gas. We hold racial opinions clandestinely, muttering them sourly among family and friends. The more desperate among us hurl racial insults (or worse) at perceived enemies from safe hiding places. And when actually called upon to own up to our ideas about "those people," we hire consultants.

It is hard to converse about anything while enraged. And the hold of habitual racism is harder to kick than heroin, particularly when practically everyone you know is a user and every newsstand and television set — projecting images of black violence in a ceaseless flow — is a pusher. We have reached the point where our racial hostility and stereotyping regenerate themselves, intensifying as if in an echo chamber, through the inertia of reciprocal resentment. Then, periodically, new and outrageous racial incidents provide this juggernaut with fresh momentum. Many African Americans now automatically presume that hostility from any white person, in any situation, is racially based. Many whites leap to the equivalent conclusion about blacks. Sometimes the facts bear out suspicions; sometimes they do not. But we can't see far enough past our own racial panic buttons to discern the difference. Americans have never been very good at this; what few skills we have gained are now rapidly being lost. Our racial screaming matches on TV and radio talk shows, for example, reflect the culture in which we live: a media-fired world of instant and effortless conclusions, in which the first and fastest information to reach our brains gains squatter's rights, and any differing point of view becomes a threatening "other."

To the extent that we tolerate this growing passivity in our racial manners, all Americans, black and white, are condemned continually to find the enmity that we seek in each other. Not that our nation's legacy of racial hate sprang from some mere whim of history, like a national bad hair day. It took several centuries of the African slave trade to sink Americans into racism. But, today, having gained a full head of hateful steam, our eagerness for ethnic bickering is cranked up to the point of making each one of us in effect racism's best friend.

Stupid? Self-defeating? Of course. Sometimes, when attacked from just the right angle, racism's very absurdity cries out for laughter. Eddie Murphy does a scathingly hilarious stand-up routine in which he recalls having snapped into the brother-with-an-attitude reflex upon arriving at a Texas airport. A helpful white luggage handler approached, asking, "Is this your bag?" Murphy whirled with centuries' worth of fury. "Yeah, it's my fucking bag!" he exploded. "What's wrong? A black man can't have a *suitcase?!*" The audience howls. It's an excruciatingly funny routine for any of us who have learned the habit of anticipating bigotry. White people claim that African Americans can be too touchy. And black people reply that we have good reason for being too touchy.

But maybe Eddie Murphy is showing us precisely the kind of conversation we need to be having. Maybe after the black passenger throws his fit, the white baggage handler grabs his arm and asks him what the hell his problem is. And the black passenger turns and replies that his problem is that a black man was dragged to his death by three white racist psychopaths less than fifty miles from here a month ago, and sometimes it's hard to tell on first sight who wants to carry your bag and who wants to spread your flesh along the pavement. The white baggage handler spits back that he doesn't want to hear it, he's sorry about the hitchhiker but *he* didn't kill him, and anyway, what good does it do anybody for the black guy to stay so paranoid? The black man replies that maybe being paranoid will, just one time in one town, save his life or spare his pride, and that maybe paranoia is still his one way of feeling in control, of feeling a step ahead of the thousand little ambushes that he knows await him in airports and on country roads. The baggage handler looks at him, thinks for a moment, and tells him that that's a hell of a way to live. The black man looks right back at him and says yeah, it sure is.

Several years ago, in France, I fell into a long conversation with a black native of the Ivory Coast who had emigrated to Paris. He quizzed me about the bizarre workings of American racism. Was it, he asked, really as cultlike as it appeared, with blacks and whites lurching in circles in the aftershocks of slavery and Jim Crow? How could we stand to live with such routine tension? He spoke of America with a mixture of wonder and horror, the way a sane man might speak of an asylum. Not that he imagined France as being racially neutral; even as he and I pondered the peculiarities of racism in the United States, we also talked about France's own rising tide of eth-

nic hatred, particularly against North African immigrants, many of whom who flee poverty and violence
in former French colonies only to find themselves jobless and stigmatized in France.

At the time of our conversation, France's racial
climate was bad; today it is worse. Economic decline
has kindled even more resentment, and in the wake of
bombings in Paris blamed on Algerian terrorists, anyone who even appears North African can be a subject
of suspicion. Hate crimes have increased. Racist and
fascist demagogues, epitomized by the rabidly anti-
immigrant Jean-Marie Le Pen, have ridden the wave
of paranoia to new heights of French electoral popularity, particularly in the south of the country. Even in
Paris, at the nation's center, a crowd of Le Pen supporters forced a North African man off a bridge into
the Seine, where he drowned.

And yet, even given the hypocrisy of France and
other nations that preach equality while practicing
their own sometimes brutal forms of repression, I
always feel, upon returning home from my trav-
els, jarred by the strangeness of American racism.
Here is where the hypocrisy is strongest. We take so
much for granted here that is, well, *weird:* the myths
of what "black" and "white" are supposed to
mean; the casual acceptance of public racial mistrust; the rest room doors of some venerable city
halls, where you can still make out "Colored" beneath four layers of paint. The only modern country

that bears comparison for sheer regimented racial lunacy is South Africa, and in some ways they are now ahead of us.

Our own long legacy of legal apartheid, based not on nationality or culture but purely on the broad fact of race, has done something peculiar to Americans. It has made our prejudices that much more irrational and crude, made our very targeting in discrimination that much less discriminating. It has given our racial judgments the look of rude childishness, as if we lack both basic manners and worldliness: Who cares where you're from? You're black/white, and I don't like you. Whether Americans see this or not, we can rest assured that the rest of the world does.

The flat-out strangeness about race in America has long made me wish that someone had written a book — as in a guidebook for tourists, or anyone who needs to be informed about the flora and fauna of a region — that could lay bare everyday racial behavior and help make sense of it. If there was a book that would help me to order lunch in Portuguese, I reasoned, then surely there ought to be a book that could assist black and white Americans in decoding racial traffic signals. This would have to be a different kind of book. It could not be an academic analysis of racism, or exclusively a work of impassioned political rhetoric; few such books hit us where we live, in the here and now, and that is precisely where we need it most. Nor could it be simply a racial memoir; racial interaction involves all of us, and can never be just one person's story. And it certainly could not be yet another pat how-to book of general, and generally useless, prescriptions; the only ones among us with all of the racial answers are the racists. What I had in mind was an engaging, accessible book that would reduce various aspects of racism to everyday essentials. I wanted a book that people could *use,* a book that would help each of us to pick our way through the minefield of racial booby traps many of us encounter each and every day. I knew of no book like it. Even as I went on with my life as a writer — publishing my first book of poems, doing readings and residencies, traveling, freelancing — the idea for such a book on race would not go away. At some point, it occurred to me that maybe I ought to try to write it.

That is where *Race Manners* came from. I wanted a book that would focus on the countless ways, great and small, we confront racism: white women clutching purses in the presence of black men; black women bristling at white women who date black men; white drivers eyeing black squeegee kids; whites backing away from racial topics because blacks seem "so sensitive"; blacks blowing off racial discussion because whites will "never understand"; telling "black" jokes; calling Elvis the King; calling him the Prince of Musical Thieves; others calling blacks ethnic while seeing whites as, well, normal; black men unsuccessfully hailing cabs; whites asking African Americans for "the black point of view." I wanted a book that would take on the more general but no less prickly matters of misunderstanding: "African American" versus "black"; affirmative action; "black" English. As many of the elements in our racial ritual of interaction and avoidance as I could.

Race Manners is personal, but I hope we are all in it: you, me, people we know. It is not a book of etiquette but a book about manners in a more basic sense: how we act around one another. I do not care how you fold your napkin. I do care very deeply about how you see me and I see you — across a table or across a subway platform — and whether we can begin to approach each other. I did not write *Race Manners* in order to bark cultural commands from on high. I offer it instead as my own ground-level window on our shared experience with race. Most of all, I mean it as a way to begin a conversation, not end it.

This book focuses on matters of black and white not for the sake of exclusivity but because, as an African American who came of age in the (literally) riotous laboratory of integration and affirmative action, I believe in writing about what I know. From my childhood amid the strivings and conflicts of the black middle class to my adult life as a poet and writer, I have come to know intimately this bizarre vibe that reverberates between black and white Americans. *Race Manners* comes from my having sat next to jittery white commuters on trains, having had interracial relationships, having felt my way through

American corporate culture, having fought with big-
ots in bars, and having stayed up late talking race
with friends, black and white. To the extent that our
black and white experiences are analogous to those of
Hispanic Americans, Asian Americans, Native Americans, and all other Americans, this book is for all
of us.

Lastly, I do not cover every topic, every situation,
every dilemma. Instead I have chosen those I think reveal much about the ways black and white Americans
think, feel, and act in one another's presence. I may
leave out things you think essential, or include things
you think inessential. That's exactly why there can be
no central authority when it comes to racial understanding, no comprehensive guidebook of universally
approved rules. There is only you and I, talking.

I heard a reporter on National Public Radio say
recently that having a dialogue with a person of another race can be more intimate than having sex. He
was talking about a town meeting on race, focusing
on Asian-American issues, but he was also talking
about racism generally. As with sex, engaging in
racial conversation today with someone you don't
know well — or even someone you do — can be
risky. And scary. Even as we feel drawn to each other,
we have rules about how much of ourselves to reveal.
And we have good reasons for caution.

But we have to talk. It is time we stopped allowing our racial conversation to be hijacked by church
bombers on the one hand and workshop leaders on

the other. Like my sister in that seminar, let's shove aside the received gospel on race and diversity. Let's dare to push toward some more honest racial reckoning in our daily lives. Let's break through the private smirks and the public taboos, and begin to get real in talking about race. If not now, when?

Getting Around

1

Typhoid Marvin: Blacks, Whites, and Public Transit

*R*ush hour on board a bus or a train. A blur of bodies, each one moving faster than thought. The flood of oncoming passengers begins to solidify. Skins jam ever closer with each stop. I am sitting next to a window, my eyes half-closed in the lurching zone between departure and arrival. Dressed conservatively in a tweed jacket and tastefully bold tie, I am an unremarkable man on an unremembered train, as unnoticed as any other commuter. Except for one thing: amid the growing crush, the seat beside me remains empty. At stop after stop, as people come on board, glance around, and seat themselves, a succession of seemingly random individual decisions* *coalesces into a glaring pattern of unoccupied spaces next to black males — including me. Soon the seats beside us are the only ones left. Other passengers remain standing, leaving these seemingly quarantined seats to those desperate souls who board once the car is choked past capacity.*

Though I have seen many white people plunk themselves down without even a glance, I have also seen, over time, a broad pattern of avoidance of black men far too pronounced for measly coincidence. Do you doubt me? Ask any black man. Better yet, begin watching.

This skirt-the-contagion dance is not a purely white set of moves. I've seen everyone do it: Asians, Hispanics, Jews, other blacks. It can run both ways. On a packed bus in a poor African-American neighborhood, a black teenager makes a grand show of avoiding the seat next to a white woman with red hair. He stops, he glares, he sits elsewhere. The woman is a friend of mine. She is regularly shunned, sneered at, and called names by black strangers when she rides buses. Some black passengers, forced to sit beside her, turn their backs on her entirely, sitting with their feet in the aisle and their bodies hunched away from her in an exaggerated pantomime of revulsion.

And so there you are in your vinyl seat: a white person treated like snow-covered carrion by perfect strangers who have dark skin. And there I am: a personable black man avoided like a jaguar by people who know nothing about me. And the question echoes between us: What in the world are we doing?

In the case of passengers avoiding black males, here is what they are doing: letting a grim fairy tale wreak havoc with what they have come to see and believe. Where does the tale come from? From the nightly news, for a start. From eerily identical television news broadcasts, each a grainy video account of poor and uneducated black men netted, like angry Discovery Channel wildebeests, by the police — another in a numbing procession of street crimes. From photographs in the local news section of sullen-looking black youths in handcuffs. From politicians who rail against a scripted cast of enemies to middle-class security: predatory criminals, savage drug addicts, hedonistic single parents who bear free-roaming young. From a dark flood of villains portrayed as disproportionately urban and black. From the lack of coverage hinting at the larger, less action-packed world in which black children do homework in tenement bedrooms and black parents marry and work long hours — and in which some white suburbanites commit felonies within stucco walls.

What Americans get from this single-themed show is a message of fear reinforced at twenty-four-hour intervals: Black inner-city people are out of control, and their kids are killers. No wonder, then, that this fear and avoidance of blacks, this tendency to give all African Americans a wide berth, has come to be second nature for so many whites.

Youth brings a nonracial component to the equation. We expect recklessness, a blind lack of restraint, from the young. And with males committing the vast majority of crimes on earth, young males, of all of our potential seatmates on buses and trains, seem most likely to be trouble.

But the young black male is special. He is our darling of perceived deviance, our poster child of ill will and bad blood. For him, we reserve special apprehension, even in the face of the facts. Consider the statistics: the vast majority of both violent and nonviolent crimes in the United States are committed by white men. While it is true that black men commit crimes at a rate greater than their percentage of the population (and we could debate the social reasons), the fact remains that on any given day any American is far more likely to suffer at the hands of a white male criminal than a black criminal. Yet somehow we manage to resist a blanket fear of white males. The double standard is stark and ugly. Many Americans, regardless of race, harbor a fear of African-American males that is wildly, even hysterically, out of proportion with reality.

And sometimes the fear can boil down to an empty seat. I know how it feels to be targeted. I have had so many seats remain empty next to me on jam-packed buses and trains that at a certain point, like many in my position, I have gone numb to the experience. I have learned to override the impulse to be maddened by the daily insult because I simply can no longer stand to care. I can no longer endure seething through innumerable bus and train rides, striving in vain to make angry eye contact with people for whom avoiding black men has become routine. I can no longer stand the prickles of paranoia, the perception of even coincidental gestures as tiny racial slights, the feeling that my ego is as accessible as public transportation.

When we hear young black urban men speak reverently of "respect," what they mean is that they are starving for the kind of casual, ordinary recognition that whites take for granted. They want what is freely given to most white strangers encountered in public: the benefits of being presumed intelligent unless proven stupid, of being presumed civilized unless shown to be otherwise, of being presumed decent unless demonstrably repellent. When this most basic of courtesies is consistently denied, the result, among legions of young black men, is an outright obsession with respect that seizes the only power available — aggression — and uses it as a weapon of self-esteem. Can't you see it on the street? The cocky walk, the expansive flinging of arms as if to claim the world, the (corporate-abetted) worship of competitive physical prowess, the idea of a gun, or of the threat of one, as hair-trigger personal veto power. "I compel, therefore I am. *Now* try to squelch my existence, punk." All in pursuit of mere acknowledgment. Such an obsession

with everyday acceptance can just as easily grip a
black commuter sheathed in a suit and tie — except
that in his case the violence coils inward. Whether by
bus or by train, it makes for a mean, and sometimes
brutally short, earthly journey.

As I've suggested with the example of my friend,
racial rejection happens to white people on buses and
trains, too. And it hurts. But there is a difference.
Most white people do not shoulder their way through
a lifetime of being singled out for hostile caricature.
And in the absence of societywide bashing of the
white self-image, they can more easily recover from
being snubbed on a bus. Black Americans are not
subject to a media barrage of images of white citizens
jacking up helpless yo boys (the dominant media messages, in fact, depict whiteness as a colorless, pleas-
antly inert state of normalcy). The "home turf"
nastiness some black passengers may show a white
commuter can best be understood as a sort of revenge. From the standpoint of many blacks, whites
have done all but beg to be disliked. To those African
Americans inclined to seek easy enemies, embracing a
raft of malignant white stereotypes (they are dirty,
they are ice-hearted, they have poor home training) can deliver the sweet rush of vindication. Black
people who have fallen victim to this influence will
seize the opportunity to make ruthlessly public their
personal distaste for white people.

Such treatment may come as a shock to some
whites. For many black Americans, however, the need

for defense against micro-assaults has long since been ingrained into our consciousness. Years of being treated as lepers in close quarters have pushed many blacks, particularly young black males, into razor-wire zones of psychic self-protection — especially in the crowded confines of a bus or train.

And so there you are: a black person or a white person avoided on public transportation. What are you supposed to do?

If you are black and angry, your first move ought to be to take a long step back from all of this ugliness. Look at the situation from a distance. Be aware that you are witnessing, in today's cultic fear of the color of your skin, a form of public insanity. When twenty-third-century historians write of the period in which we now live — in much the same way that historians now view, say, the ordeals of free blacks during the era of legalized slavery in America — they will judge such behavior with sadness and some measure of disbelief.

Take the clinical view for a moment. The whites who avoid sitting next to you know squat about you as a person, and worse, they don't know that they know squat. Like many nonblack Americans who have little experience with black people, they believe the media distortions about who you are alleged to be. And if they have had even one bad personal experience with an African American, they are prone to embrace the resulting image for life. Psychiatrists tag substituting exaggerated fears for reality as classically delusional. Should you be offended if a procession of diagnosed paranoid schizophrenics refuses to sit beside you on a bus? People who entertain sensational preconceptions of you fall into an analogous category of lunacy, if only for a few moments at a time. So treat them as lunatics. Sit back, read your newspaper, or look out of the window, and marvel at a world that regularly offers you extra seating room.

Still not satisfied? Want to fight back? You might consider some preemptive moves of your own. For example, place your jacket or satchel on the empty seat next to you, forcing anyone who wants the seat to request it. Sit on the aisle side, effectively blocking the empty window seat until someone asks whether they can slide in. Or make it a habit to sit only beside other people. Such gyrations of self-protection, though, might seem weak and hollow. To what extent, after all, are you really willing to allow other people's behavior to govern your own?

If, on the other hand, you are a black person who singles out white passengers for isolation or abuse, you can claim the dubious distinction of having assisted in your own dehumanization. Your collaboration in fanning racial ill will among perfect strangers helps to lower black political consciousness to its shallowest possible level — that is, to the same level of blind ethnic belligerence as white supremacism. With your continued assistance, this state of racial barbarism will continue indefinitely.

To many whites, the mere fact of their seatmate

preferences on buses and trains may come as jarring news. How are they supposed to notice patterns so universal as to seem invisible? Freedom from such awareness, after all, comes with being white. American Caucasians can spend their entire lives dancing away from young black males and never even realize it. If you are white, chances are fairly good that you have already done so. Nobody would call you a bad person for doing something of which you are unaware. But if you don't *want* to know, that's another story. So now you've been told. When you take public transit, pay attention. What you see may surprise you.

When and if you find yourself disinclined to sit beside a young black male on a bus or a train, ask yourself this: if he were of a different race (with the identical manner, clothing, expression, etc.) would you sit down beside him without hesitating? If your answer is no, then avoid him guilt-free. But if the answer is yes, you have a problem. There are plenty of perfectly good reasons for not wanting to sit beside someone: ripe body odor; a rancorous, twisted smile; an open bottle; the demeanor of a just-opened vein. But a person's age, race, and gender simply do not cut it as warning signs. Every time your unthinking prejudice makes me or anyone else an involuntary representative of scariness, you hurt the feelings — and raise the blood pressure — of a human being who deserves better. You become, in effect, an unwitting apostle for some of the more boorish beliefs burdening our planet. This is antisocial behavior at its worst. Change it.

If you're white and find yourself persona non grata on a largely black bus or train route, with passengers emitting potently noxious signals for your benefit, you should try, like young black males caught in similar social ambushes, to treat this as you would any other bizarre compulsion. You can defend yourself, if you choose, by guarding the empty seat beside you. But such petty relief is strictly stopgap. Are you really willing to play cat and mouse on buses and trains forever? Would it not be better to understand what looms behind the rage: a siege mentality to which many African Americans have succumbed, one in which they judge all whites as broadly and as harshly as they themselves feel judged? As a white person, you can escape abuse by getting off the bus. For black Americans, it is not so easy.

2

Survival and Stereotype:
On the Street and in Public

A *white couple walks after dark on a city side-walk. Approaching are two young black males, walking side by side, in baggy clothing. They could be high school seniors with B-minus averages and new haircuts, heading to a girlfriend's birthday party. They could be high school dropouts, minnows in the street-drug food chain, carrying cheap guns because their rivals carry cheap guns. They could be cousins who work the late shift together at McDonald's. The white couple does not know who these young men are, but they feel afraid: the baggy clothes, the big shoes, the swaggering walk. Danger. Get back to the ship, Will Robinson! The white couple wonders what to do: Cross the street? Turn around? No other pedestrians are nearby. The two young black men see their fear and sneer. They laugh to themselves at the fright movie playing behind the white couple's frozen stare. Twenty feet. Ten feet. Cold eyes meet cold eyes.*

Cut to broad daylight. A black man (he sells office supplies) enters an elevator and stands next to a white female stranger (she sells insurance). Instantly, as if cued, she tightens her hold on her purse, locking her elbow inward for a better grip. She doesn't think about it. She just does it. She has never had her purse snatched. She does, however, watch a lot of television. Seven months from now, as it turns out, she will be robbed — accosted from behind by a white man. But right now, gripping her purse tightly, all she knows is that she is within the reach of this black man.

Or: A white man (he keeps a company's books) quickly reaches to pat his own wallet pocket just after a black man (he is a well-known musician) starts to pass him on the street. The gesture is subtle. Reflexive. Unmistakable. It's something the white bookkeeper does several times a day in public. The black musician sees him do it. He sees white men do it many times a day in his presence. The white man sees the black man see him. The moment passes. The black musician manages to refrain, though just barely, from making a mockingly exaggerated attempt to pick the white man's pocket.

Cut to a poor white neighborhood at dusk. The inhabitants are what an elderly black lady might lower her voice to call "poor white trash." You are a black man traveling on foot who did not plan to be here. But here you are. Four young white men in tank tops and T-shirts stand on a stoop. They stop talking in order to look at you. They could be old friends only momentarily distracted from their jovial business. They could be jobless, drunk, and eager to kick some goddamned nigger's ass. They could be merely cautious, sensing you sensing them. You don't know who they are, but you think you recognize them: faces from Bensonhurst and South Boston and every other white urban neighborhood from which a black man has failed to return. And now they are watching you watch them, and they are silent.

What a way to travel. Too often, our worst habits and fantasies masquerade as intuition. We strain our eyes looking for color and in the process lose all our other senses. Yet the stakes seem too high to exercise anything other than fear — to grip our purses, to check for our wallets, to prepare to fight or run. Do we bruise sensibilities? Make bigoted presumptions? "Well," we say, "too bad." Just as on subways and buses, it is not always a simple matter of whites stereotyping blacks and vice versa. Some especially potent coded fears are embraced by blacks and whites alike, particularly along class lines. One middle-class black woman declared to me her automatic avoidance of young black males on the street at night: "Hey, sorry, but I'm making it home *alive.*"

But racial images are at their most fearsome when we stray into an unfamiliar neighborhood. America's brutal history has taught us all well. In many communities — sometimes divided by only a street — blacks or whites can feel like trespassers, fiercely alert for even the slightest scent of blood on the wind. Today's racial climate has even further heightened the air of fear.

These are not happy times for many Americans — poor, working class, or middle class. Many whites have seen their standards of living plummet and their economic security evaporate, their expectations shrunk by disposable short-term jobs. They are embittered that the opportunity for prosperity, much ballyhooed during the cresting of the stock market in the past decade, has eluded their grasp. Many blacks have seen inner-city communities decline from poverty into outright crisis while their own government imprisons more and more black men and relaxes its efforts against poverty and discrimination. They feel betrayed as never before.

The search for blame is feverish: it's the lazy blacks; it's single mothers; it's white racists bent on annihilating African Americans; it's greedy Jews; it's swarming illegal immigrants; it's godlessness; it's affirmative action; it's government.

There is only one sure way out of this funhouse:

discard your preconceptions, rescue your basic instincts for distinguishing real threats from false clues (instead of yielding to the grip of cultural stereotyping), and learn how to use and trust your ability to see what is happening around you. No matter how hard it is, forget the television news, or your friend's having been robbed, or your having had "nigger" yelled at you from a jacked-up Trans Am in East Baltimore. You do not live in a scripted scene from TV, and you do not live in your past. You live among people who are who they are, not who you try to conceive them to be. If you have good reason — based on local experience or concrete advice — to exercise care, then do so. Do the "don't-fuck-with-me" walk. Be alert. But also admit that there is a lot about the people around you that you just do not know. And most of the time, paranoia will only blind you.

I know this is even harder than it sounds, given that in our thickening atmosphere of racial hatred whites and blacks are encouraged to approach each other bristling with hostile presumptions. A prerecorded sound track of canned racial clichés, like personal elevator music, renders us deaf to the world. Like figures in B movies or slasher films, we become possessed by scripts — "that black man might try for my purse," "that white woman is going to cringe when I get on this elevator." We never reach the point of comparing actual events with our preconceptions because we never get past our preconceptions.

But here is the hard part: these preconceptions

are based on truth as well as fantasy. White pedestrians *have* been attacked by groups of vengeful black youths. A black man *was* dragged from a pickup truck in Texas until his arms and legs came off. White commuters *have* been shot execution-style on trains. Black teenagers *have* been chased and killed by mobs in depressed white communities.

Yet it is possible for me as a black man to make my casual way through any number of white neighborhoods on the strength of my routine attentiveness to what is going on around me — without being paralyzed by fear that I am about to be strung up and castrated. Black men do it every day without ending up on the evening news. It is just as feasible for whites to travel through most black neighborhoods without having to run for their lives.

Gavin DeBecker, an expert on dealing with the threat of violence and author of *The Gift of Fear,* has warned against using race as a sign of danger when what really matters is a person's actions — a set of behavioral cues he calls "pre-incident indicators." People who judge strangers by race, he says, hinder their own ability to recognize threats that have nothing to do with ethnicity.

The only antidote to prefabricated racial hysteria is for us all to come to our senses, to reclaim common sense from reflexive panic and fury. In the end, our only real personal protection — our best hope for preserving our humanity, as well as our skins, whether on a back road or a packed city street — lies in our ability to see, hear, think, and act clearly. There are indeed threats against which we need to protect ourselves. But locking ourselves into a stance of rigid defensiveness makes us no safer. Like a boxer who hides behind his gloves, terrified of giving his opponent an opening, we await and assure our own defeat.

So what should you do on the street? Pay attention. Are people eyeing you or ignoring you? Is that really a hostile group of characters hovering in your vicinity, or are you *interpreting* a black teenager in a sweat suit, or a group of white men in T-shirts leaning against a car, as hostile? What kinds of expressions do you read on people's faces? How do they act after you have passed them?

There are of course blocks and whole neighborhoods where, whether due to racial tension or a high crime rate in general, you simply don't want to be, at least not alone. There are many more areas where anyone can walk unmolested, perhaps even unnoticed. Exercise the usual care; brightly lit or crowded places are obviously safer than isolated or darkened ones. Learn about your surroundings in advance. Fear and vulnerability are like loud clothing: they make you an obvious mark. A rule of thumb is that if you are not able to move with a reasonable amount of self-assurance in a given setting, you don't belong there. You yourself can judge what a "reasonable amount" is. Whatever you do, base your actions on what is actually happening, and on nothing more. Or you may attract precisely the attention that you most fear.

If you are white, here is a little tip: black Americans are far more accustomed to being around you than you are to being around them. Sheer numbers force nearly every African American to interact regularly with whites, while, as you probably know, there are many whites who spend little or no significant time around black people. Many black people therefore know you better than you know them. Your presence in their lives or in their neighborhoods is not as worthy of notice as you might think. Don't flatter yourself into believing that you're a bigger attraction than you are. Be prepared to react, as you would in any situation, when the feeling is bad and you have the sense of being a target. But treat any black neighborhood as what it is: a community, with a variety of people and attitudes. Just like a white neighborhood.

If you are black and trying to keep paranoia in check, you would do well to remember that time-worn moral: Don't do them the way that they do us. You have learned, justifiably, to have a hair-trigger reaction when it comes to white racism, and to expect flagrant and sometimes violent bigotry from some whites. The redneck stereotype of poor whites is a potent one among many blacks, as are countless other generalizations and suspicions. But think about how crazy it makes you to hear white suburbanites prattle on about "those people" — by which they mean you, your friends, and your family. Do you really want to adopt such a system of belief? Are you really so fragile that you need to sheathe yourself in a preemptive dislike of whites, or huddle in constant fear of rejection or anger? As black people, we can protect ourselves perfectly well from bodily and psychological attack without needing to skulk through life, claws extended and hair standing on end.

Once, in San Francisco, while my cousin and I were standing at a crosswalk, a white woman in the nearest car looked at us nervously, then conspicuously leaned over and locked her door. I flinched, as if stung, and made a sarcastic remark to my cousin, who glanced at me and in his typically laconic way said, "Who cares? She's worried. I'm not." Then he changed the subject. I stared at him, dumbfounded by his offhand denial of what I felt certain must have gnawed at his gut the way it gnawed at mine. But then it began to register: he really didn't care. I was the one incapacitated by some stranger's display of fear. I had in fact looked at her, which is why I noticed her reaction to us in the first place. I remember having said to myself, "I'll bet she locks her car door." And, as if to fulfill my prophesy, she did. Was it my fault that she was afraid? No. Was it because I was male? Possibly. Was it because I was black and male? Likely.

But whatever the case, my preoccupation with her perception of me — my need to see how she saw me — was a surrender of self. What if instead I had been too busy talking with my cousin, too busy being who I am, to have been affected by someone's peripheral paranoia? I would have served myself instead of her. Black men need to know how to do this. Allowing the momentary hijacking of our sense of self by random acts of fear or hate — call it guerrilla racism — is bad for us. Literally. The high rates of hypertension, stroke, and heart disease among African-American men bear brutal witness to the problem. Do not volunteer yourself as a casualty. Let those with the illness, those who caricature and misrepresent you, be the ones consumed.

My older sister recalls a conversation she once had with an elderly black woman about handling personal incidents of racism. The older woman told her how, some years earlier, she and several black female friends were sightseeing in a southern city when a car full of white youths roared alongside, yelled "Nigger!" and other epithets, and sped off. The woman finished her story by remarking, placidly, that she and her friends had gone on to have a perfectly marvelous afternoon. My sister, astonished at the woman's composure, asked, "But didn't the episode with the white boys completely wreck your day?" The woman gave her a surprised look. "Why should it? It was pure foolishness."

We could stand to bear this in mind.

3

Traffic Patterns

The Black Man's Burden: Hailing a Cab

Being a black male trying to hail a taxicab in Manhattan is like, well, being a black male trying to hail a taxicab in Manhattan. Which is to say, brutal and humiliating. The experience could be packaged and sold on the market as a therapeutic toughening-up course for weaklings: boot camp for rejection. If enlisting in the marines builds character, being black and uptown-bound on a Manhattan curb will build a titan. You're neatly dressed, pressed for time — and invisible. Cab after empty cab barrels by. Some even swerve to avoid you. Meanwhile, white patrons on either side of you clamber happily into taxis. You feel like a chump for having placed yourself here, at the mercy of fleeting yellow vehicles accelerating through your ego.

You might be ready to put a brick through the impassive eye of a windshield.

You might stop, amid the noise, and consider your options.

For black American males, hailing a cab is such a classic problem as to have entered the realm of folk-lore. Everyone has a story. Even such figures as social thinker Cornel West and former New York City mayor David Dinkins have suffered the indignity — as have I and most other black men — of watching taxis pick up white customers left and right, while pointedly refusing to stop for them. Simply put, taxi-cab drivers (many of them black, by the way) are afraid of black males, whether clad in Nike sweats or Barney's suits. One black female cabdriver of my ac-quaintance who works the Baltimore metropolitan area told me that every robbery or scary incident she has ever experienced in her cab — and they number in the dozens — has involved a young black man. No exceptions. She was blunt and unapologetic: "I won't pick them up. Not anymore. It's not worth it."

Of course, this is a big country. The last time I was in Sheridan, Wyoming, there was little evidence that black males ranked high on cabdrivers' list of characters to avoid — mostly because there was little evidence of black males, period. But if you are a black man trying to flag down a taxi in New Haven, Atlanta, or Los Angeles, you are up against unfriendly odds.

The free-roaming black criminal, like the escaped slave of centuries past, is a demonic icon for our time. Modern legend has him stalking the innocent mainstream with deadly, silken moves. In the merciless rush of city traffic, where decisions about whom to pick up and whom to avoid are made at lightning speed, a black man on a street corner with his arm upraised becomes, in a split second, representative of the last dozen black men seen being hauled away in the backs of squad cars on television. Give him a ride? Not in this life.

All of which means that if you are a black man who is neither driving nor chauffeured, your options are limited. There is no way, short of flinging your body into traffic, to force an unwilling cabbie to stop.

But if you are inclined to fight back, here are a few tactics worth trying. One is to position yourself near a white person who began hailing a cab after you did. When a taxi stops for him or her, run over and call out that you were hailing a cab first. When the driver of the stopped cab sees what is happening, he may sputter non sequiturs while escaping back into traffic, but you will at least have made flagrant discrimination slightly less comfortable for all concerned.

Another technique is to approach one of the white taxi-hailers and straightforwardly explain the situation. This, too, is a long shot (your mere approach may scare him off), but an occasional robust soul may take some conspiratorial pleasure in helping you to gain your overdue ride.

Such small triumphs can be sweet. On one occasion, in Manhattan, when I was in a frantic hurry to get to the train station and had trouble getting a cab, a Japanese-American friend who was seeing me off actually stepped in and hailed one for me. I will never forget the expression of incredulity on the cabbie's face when I jumped into his backseat alone, waved good-bye to my friend, and barked, "Penn Station." In another instance, a black male in-law of mine, incensed when a Manhattan cabbie refused to take him uptown, ran around the cab in a rage and opened all of its doors in the middle of traffic while raining Ivy League invective upon the taxi driver. It did not get my in-law any closer to his destination. It did, however, grant him a moment's satisfaction.

But short of cursing or scheming, the best — and saddest — solution is to find ways to avoid cabs. In cities such as New York and Washington, D.C., where taxis are infamously discriminatory, I use public transportation at every opportunity. Calling a car service (one that knows your destination ahead of time) can also provide an alternative. Why pay cabbies for ritual abuse?

You might instead write letters of protest to cab companies and to taxi commissions, and encourage others to do the same. Or spread word of a possible boycott. One enterprising group of Washington, D.C., law students actually filed suit — and collected damages — against a local taxi firm after the students videotaped a "sting" operation in which cabbies openly discriminated against black would-be passengers. There is, clearly, more than one way to skin a cab.

Race Through a Windshield: Squeegee Kids and You

A line of traffic. A red light. Preadolescent black boys, squeegees or sponges in hand, rush for stopped cars. A few drivers nod their heads for a quick (if not always thorough) windshield cleaning for spare change. Others refuse. You know this scene: the boys, some engaging, others sullen, are all busy seizing the fleeting opportunity of this traffic-light cycle's captive market. The nearest adults are seated behind automotive safety glass. Some drivers are palpably nervous, as if idling their engines among young wolves, fingers tapping on the steering wheel, waiting for the light to change. Windows go up. Door locks click. This is as close as some commuters ever come to the faces and hands of black inner-city kids. For some, it is too close. Is it too close for you?

It is too easy to slam as twitchy yo-phobia any driver's caution in the presence of squeegee kids. It is also too easy to bleat disingenuously about a driver's right to privacy and personal space, as if race and class were not crucial ingredients here. When apple-cheeked blond boys flag down suburban traffic for Cub Scout car washes, few car doors lock.

So let's spare each other the self-righteous dogma. Scary things *do* happen at city stoplights, and some squeegee kids, like all hell-bent young capitalists, make a point of putting their propositions directly in your face. They have taken a good lesson, in fact, from America's mainstream marketers: apply enough pressure with an offer, and even the most resistant customers will eventually cave in. So there is ample reason for any driver to be wary, annoyed, or defensive when subject to unwelcome attention at a traffic light. The real question for drivers is whether the in-your-face pubescent audacity is what unnerves them, or the face itself: that of a black child with whom they might never otherwise share space.

To be sure, one dimension of the dread of squeegee kids is the fear of strangers in general. We live in times when ordinary-looking customers in fast-food restaurants suddenly open fire with semiautomatic weapons, when expressionless children mow down classmates without warning. For many drivers, the die-cast and enameled shelter of a car — epitomized by the heavy, big-tired sport utility vehicles that are now all the rage — feels like the only available protection in a landscape prowled by monsters. Clicking the door lock and rolling up the window, like pressing the TV remote midway through a prime-time murder, is a way of trying to control the threat.

But who is the enemy? How do you decide, from

your driver's seat, who is dangerous and who is not? From experience? Or from less reliable impulses? In all of my years of driving in New York, Baltimore, Los Angeles, and other big cities, my worst experience with a squeegee kid has been coming away with a muddy windshield. This isn't to say that your experience wouldn't differ. Maybe my being black and male affects some of the dynamics. Maybe my being careful makes a difference. Maybe I'm lucky. I cannot entirely know. Neither can you.

Not that I have evaded all street-corner traffic scams. Late one night as I sat in my car at a clogged Baltimore intersection, I was approached by a man carrying a gasoline can. He begged me for spare change so that he could put enough gas in his car to get home. He was earnest and pathetic. When I refused to give him money he seemed beside himself with frustration. Later I felt guilty about it — until I saw him on subsequent nights at the same intersection with the same gasoline can. He was one of the slickest con artists I have ever seen. He was white.

What if the driver is you? Whether you're white or black, be nervous, if you must, about real rather than imagined dangers. Are you the only car at the traffic light at a notoriously dangerous corner after dark? Is a group of grim-looking kids converging on your car as if they intend to attack more than your windshield? Carjackings and purse snatchings happen; you would be naive not to be wary when someone approaches you in traffic.

But if you routinely tremble in the presence of kids armed with squeegees, consider who is really at greatest risk of harm: the children themselves, who too tragically often fail to emerge safely from traffic. Driven by joblessness into the path of your car, they, not you, are the true casualties.

And if you can't stop worrying about being attacked, try to look at it from a would-be attacker's point of view. If you have stealing a purse or hijacking a car in mind, are you going to lug a bucket to a busy street corner and plant yourself, sponge in hand, in front of a parade of potential witnesses before making your move? As capers go, it seems like a low-percentage strategy.

As with homelessness and panhandling — which, due to poverty, also involve a disproportionate number of black people — the issue of squeegee kids has been popularly reduced to a matter of mere public nuisance. What tends to get lost in all the city-hall jabbering about crime and delinquents and quality of life is that the street-corner squeegee business began as an ingenious little enterprise, one example among many ("selling" parking spaces for tips is another) of the cleverness and creativity of young black kids who, given the shrinking market in low-wage jobs and the burgeoning street-drug trade, have few legal options for making money. Why not give them your business? Better yet, why not push for the kind of social change that will help to generate jobs?

Seeing the World

4

Till O. J. Do Us Part: Our Separate and Unequal Brushes with the Law

*T*he police. Charged with serving, protecting, and occasionally, ticketing. Their job is to keep an eye out for trouble in your neighborhood. Or maybe, if you're black, to keep an eye out for you in neighborhoods where they think you don't belong. The police. They hand you a traffic summons and tell you to have a nice day. Or maybe, if you're black, they whale on you with nightsticks, kick you into a fetal ball, then order you to stand up. The police. They respond to our calls for help and retrieve our stolen cars and maintain what's left of the peace. Or maybe, if you're black, they keep you perched *alertly on your tailbone when you catch that glint of blue or red flashing in your rearview mirror.*

It's crazy, think some whites: all these African Americans with their preconditioned rage toward the police, who, after all, look after the property and safety of black folks, too. It's crazy, think some blacks: all these whites living in utter denial of the spectacular brazenness with which police reserve special scrutiny — and abuse — for black people.

Well, somebody's *crazy.*

What is crazy is our society's smug civic pretense of a single standard of law enforcement when in fact blacks and whites live on opposite sides of a practically impermeable divide. Call it the Melanin Curtain — a magically fluid but durable veil through which, say, a middle-class black woman browsing in a jewelry store becomes, to the eye of a security guard, a smartly dressed thief. The same veil makes her white counterpart invisible, unworthy of notice. Whether a matter of traffic citations or felony arrests, the problem is not that blacks or whites as groups are lying when they recite contradictory histories of their treatment at the hands of the police. The problem is that they are both telling the truth.

If you are white, the first thing you need to understand is that black people are not making this stuff up. You need to try to imagine living in a parallel universe in which the public invisibility that you and many other whites take for granted is denied. The racial double standard in law enforcement is not some self-excusing concoction on the part of black Americans. It is as real as the sudden hook of a siren or a sudden yank at the neck. Get used to this idea: actual people in actual encounters with the law are seen and treated differently because of skin color, with a consistency etched in the statistics.

In New York City — where crime is falling, while complaints of police brutality are rising — two-thirds of the victims of police violence were members of racial minorities, according to a 1996 Amnesty International report. The 1997 incident in which New York City police officers tortured Haitian immigrant Abner Louima with a toilet plunger was an extreme example, but not an anomaly. A Human Rights Watch report released in 1998, reflecting two years of research in fourteen American cities, found that minorities alleged police brutality with a frequency far out of proportion with their percentage of the population. The report noted that data on brutality can be hard to obtain due to police secrecy, but it concluded from available evidence that "police have subjected minorities to apparently discriminatory treatment," including abuses that violate international standards for human rights.

Similarly, the War on Drugs — some African Americans call it the War on Blacks — created a battle-zone mentality by disproportionately targeting blacks, though whites continued to make up the vast majority of illegal drug users. According to a report by University of Minnesota criminologist Michael Tonry, between 1980 and 1990 the proportion of blacks among those arrested for drug offenses ballooned from 24 to 41 percent, and the proportion of blacks among those incarcerated in state and federal prisons rose from 39 to 53 percent.

At street level, all this means a world of difference between the black and the white experience with the law. For example, the use of "profiles" to troll for suspected criminals in public places has become standard among badly outgunned and underfunded narcotics detectives. The profile is pretty basic. If you are black, male, casually dressed, and look under fifty, be prepared to attract police attention. At a major metropolitan train station a few years ago, after returning home from a business trip to New York, I was surrounded and quizzed by white undercover detectives to whom I appeared to "fit the profile" — their words — for drug trafficking. When I took my complaint to the city's black chief prosecutor, he sighed. He was familiar with the clash between overwhelmed detectives and the rights of citizens. He told me his own stories about having been repeatedly stopped and questioned while in college and law school by white police officers who found him "suspicious." He was more than just sympathetic. He was upset by my allegations, and promised to investigate and to push the chief of police into demanding that detectives exhibit more judicious behavior. The prosecutor (he has since become mayor) kept his word. As part of the fallout from my case, the (black) supervisor of the three detectives came to my office and personally apologized.

Chances are that within a week or two another law-abiding black person was accosted by the same detectives. Apologies are well and good for those fortunate enough to have contacts (a friend was an assistant prosecutor in this city), but the fact remains that the Supreme Court has found using profiles as an excuse to stop and search people to be constitutional. Every day, countless black citizens — who like everyone want the simple freedom to move in public unmolested — are detained and interrogated by police, not because they fit the description of a particular suspect but because they look to police like the kind of people who might turn out to be suspects. Which is to say, black.

The American Civil Liberties Union (ACLU) has, for example, recently filed a class-action lawsuit on behalf of minority motorists detained by the Maryland State Police along Interstate 95. The suit grew out of a 1993 lawsuit on behalf of a Harvard-educated black lawyer and his family, who for no apparent reason were stopped and searched on the highway. The ACLU alleges a long-term pattern of discrimination in racial profiling by state police. According to the police department's own figures, during a three-year period more than 75 percent of drivers stopped and searched on Interstate 95 were African Americans or members of other minority groups. If you are white, you may find such numbers surprising. If you are black, you won't.

It's not just a male thing. Ask black women who have pulled years or decades of jail time for such minor drug infractions as being in the car with someone who carried drugs. Ask black women about being watched and followed in stores. Some fight back. My favorite example comes from a story told by a middle-class black woman. After being followed in an expensive store, she went to the counter as if to make a purchase and instead loudly ordered the manager to cancel her charge account, then told him why.

I am not saying that a black person should be excused from any justified suspicion. But the justification is one's actions, not one's race. When I was in college, several classmates and I, all black, made it a habit to steal anything we could get our hands on from a nearby convenience store. We were never caught. We wore long coats and walked out with boxes of doughnuts, loaves of bread, six-packs of soft drinks. We didn't steal because we couldn't afford food. We stole because, as budding college radicals, we fancied ourselves to be striking small blows against capitalist authority. Did we deserve suspicion? Would we have deserved to be treated like thieves on the basis of our actions? Absolutely. But we deserved it no more than a certain white friend of mine. He was the first expert shoplifter I ever met.

When it comes to race, your economic class, normally an effective American trump (it might insulate a white suburbanite from police crudities such as public handcuffing or pistol-whipping) is often useless. Viewed through the Melanin Curtain, even a rich black person at certain moments has no personal assets except one: blackness. "Just-another-nigger" stories crowd the landscape. Legendary jazz musician Miles Davis remained bitter until his death about the frequency with which police pulled him over in his Ferrari for questioning. News accounts (often carried only in the black press) surface regularly of well-known black figures skirmishing with police officers who mistook them for "ordinary" (i.e., criminal) black folk in wealthy communities. Police on prosperous Mercer Island, Washington State, made news recently because of their practice of routinely stopping and questioning everyone and anyone who is black. For every brightly lit story in Brentwood or Beverly Hills, there are a thousand more that take place in the nation's shadows.

Which brings us to that most notorious of black suburban fugitives, O. J. Simpson. He is where black and white ideas about police go to war. We can argue forever about whether O. J. did it or not. Those who believe he is guilty can forever express their shock over the jury's stunning ability to ignore overwhelmingly incriminating evidence. Those who think he is innocent can endlessly proclaim that the evidence was fixed and the prosecution tainted. But as an explanation of the verdict and its aftermath, such righteous fury completely misses the point. The storm over the trial was about something much deeper and broader than one man's innocence or guilt. The real meaning of the O. J. trial, for many blacks who fervently wished for his acquittal, was not so much that they wanted him to win. It was that they wanted the police to lose.

Simpson's victory was due partly to legal genius, partly to his goofy "good Negro" megacelebrity, and partly to prosecutorial weakness. But what really saved O. J. from life (or death) in the cell block was the Los Angeles Police Department's notorious legacy of racism — as supported by revelations about key officers in the trial — and the consuming desire in the African-American community for justice for the city's untold thousands of brutalized black men.

In the mere fact of being a prominent black male murder defendant in a city with such a history, O. J. Simpson hit the jackpot. In the wake of the Rodney King beating and the subsequent criminal acquittal of its videotaped perpetrators, no jury in Los Angeles with any black members was going to send this chuckling, amiable black football star to jail, whatever the evidence and whatever his history. Take it as a testimony to the depth of black frustration that many African Americans should choose so unlikely a beneficiary as O. J. Simpson — a man with little apparent attachment to any community of blackness — for their efforts. Is it scary that so many black Americans are this desperate for racial justice? Yes.

And so, particularly if you are white, you need to

realize that the world of many black Americans is one in which a blue uniform represents something shatteringly different from what it represents in your world. Some individual black people may crank up the volume about police villainy purely for personal or political effect, but the physical and psychological damage done by the double standard of America's police forces is as real as a corpse. Any honest racial conversation about the law has to begin there. If you are looking for truth, for some real understanding of what is happening racially between us, you have to start listening to what black people are saying. This doesn't mean you have to buy every story, be it that of Tawana Brawley or O. J. Simpson. But it does mean that you have to be open to truths that defy your own experience.

And if you are black, you need to recognize that most whites are not conspiring to deny the facts as you know them. They are not malevolently embracing a skewed view of the world, nor forcibly blinding themselves through sheer mean-spiritedness to the smoldering history between blacks and cops. Instead, most whites are like you: decent, well-intentioned people acting within the limitations of their own experience. Moreover, many poor whites know a great deal about the hard and ugly edge of the law. But the relatively insulated mass of white middle America simply has no direct knowledge of the dramas played out just offstage, beyond their peripheral vision. To them, your vast and varied experience as a black person takes place in a void, somewhere beyond the edge of the earth, a place they can envision only through TV-beamed images, mostly of black criminals and cops.

You do not need to shoulder responsibility for widening such a white person's scope. You do, however, need to resist treating whites as mythical characters in their own right — as pernicious creatures of prejudice who hungrily collect and covet racial poisons, even as they cheer on the police. You know better. If you expect to be heard, you ought to treat people as if they are capable of listening.

In *Warrior's Honor,* Michael Ignatieff's collection of essays about ethnic war, he writes of hiding in a cellar in Croatia with a Serb soldier who, through trading gunfire with former neighbors and friends, has jettisoned his prior identity in favor of a harder and simpler one: Serb. And so, writes Ignatieff, "because he is only a Serb for his enemies, he has become only a Serb to himself."

5

The Extraterrestrial's Guide to Hate

I'll confess something: I have never really understood hate. Yes, I grew up in America. Yes, I have had epithets screamed at me from people in moving cars, witnessed — and been in — racial brawls; heard landlords lie through their teeth about vacancies; watched guys yank themselves away from an apparently good time with their friends in a bar simply to vent their fury at my presence. I know rage and some of its sources: abuse, lost faith, broken promises, powerlessness. I know the drill on hate, and so perhaps do you. But somehow I just can't envision being down in the works of the thing. Hate is such hard work. It is exhausting, punishing, and constant, an exercise in desperation and perennial defeat.*

I try to imagine what that must be like for a racist. I mean a serious *racist, someone who is sick with it, sour with it, like a razor-edged belch; someone who passes out pamphlets calling for a bloody end to this or that group; someone who chews constantly on his own anger; someone who feels perpetually threatened by racial enemies; someone who murders a complete stranger for the sake of a tattoo. What does such a person feel like from the inside? What could congeal a soul in such a hellish state? I walk into a diner out in the country and see a white person turn away from a heaping plate of hot food to glare long and hard at me, and I wonder: what is it like behind those hooded eyes, at the moment when the hated "other" looms in their field of vision?*

What was it like for those people in Rochester, New York — I don't know for certain who they were, but I have an idea — who signed the petition protesting my family's moving into our new house in a white neighborhood? What was it like to be that drunken white man in dirty clothes who thrust out his leg as if to trip me, a black stranger in a business suit, as I walked past him on a bus? What is it like for black kids who lie in wait to pummel any white stranger who happens to come along?

I don't know. Chances are you don't either; if you did, you would not have this book in your hand; you would have flung it across the room or, more likely, left it on the shelf. But I'll tell you what we do know, you and I: we know that the anger thickens our very air in the places where we live. It crackles on car radios; it electrifies glares among black and white strangers at malls; it forges our own shoulder-squaring readiness for ambush. We know that strangers feel more and more like potential enemies. And we know that all of this leaves us less room, somehow, to move with ease, let alone joy.

Before my father suffered a crippling stroke, he had other ways of venting his rage. I remember the way that he had, when I was a child, of dealing with hateful white stares when we walked down a street. He would abruptly turn toward our scrutinizers and freeze, feet spread like a boxer's, hands on hips, eyes locked on the offending parties in a searing glare, as if to declare, "I stand to judge you." The watchers saw his defiance. What they did not see was the way that, at home, he cried.

Hate is a set of worming gears out there as big as the world. It constantly, mindlessly grinds at black and white men and women, reduces them to wounded flesh, spits them forth as skin desperadoes. And some of them want to hurt you, and others want to hurt me. They live among us and within us. Some carry live ammunition. How can we survive with our hearts intact?

It might help if we tried to see all of this from an alien's point of view. Say, a blue-skinned Venusian from a completely nonaggressive culture. Let's suppose that a series of seismic shifts is slowly but steadily lowering parts of the coastline of Venus's single continent into the ocean, gradually displacing hundreds of thousands into the already overcrowded interior. A treaty with the United States — which covets Venusian technological skills — allows some of these refugees to emigrate. With no room on Venus, they've little choice but to accept the offer of safe passage to America. But it means leaving the peace of Venusian tradition — in which trust among complete strangers has been the norm for millennia — for an American way of life riddled with bizarre conflicts and fears. Chief among these, as blared in the Venusian tabloids, is the American spectacle of race.

In this new place where neither his azure skin nor his automatic empathy with strangers is taken in stride, the newly arrived Venusian is in dire need of sound advice. Fortunately, as part of the briefing process, a Venusian government committee of experts has prepared a series of handy brochures for prospective emigrants, including one on adapting to the racial biases of Americans. The Venusian gets his hands on a copy.

The Venusian's Guide, Vol. 24: Habits of Race in America

Welcome to Earth and its most aggressive culture, the United States. As part of your early adjustment, you MUST familiarize yourself with important rules governing the social behavior of Americans. In this pocket guide, you will find information that will help you to begin to understand and befriend Americans — a convivial people at heart — without falling victim to their chief weaknesses. READ THIS GUIDE. It will spare you painful — or dangerous — social errors.

Cardinal Custom: Americans sort people by skin color, which they call "race." They base their reactions (warmth, hostility, trust, mistrust) to strangers not chiefly on behavior but on skin hue and other "racial" traits. The prejudice has a pattern — the lighter the better (with some variations for hair, eyes, and facial features) — and the custom stems from a recent system of captive labor for profit, in which skin color was used as an explanation for enslavement. Many Americans remain vague about the facts of this enterprise; you will find the darkest-skinned Americans (descendants of the formerly enslaved, originally from civilizations on a continent known as Africa) the most willing to discuss its peculiar history.

Prepare. Racial prejudice is unlike any custom you have ever encountered. It contradicts all of your instincts, as a Venusian, about what to expect from others. Among strangers in the United States, fear is the rule rather than warmth and trust (see vol. 9, *Property and Crime*) and race is its chief symbol. Despite your special citizenship under the Treaty, in informal interactions your blue skin may place you toward the bottom of the American skin scale. You will meet with suspicion in public places, be more carefully scrutinized during transactions, have more trouble renting or purchasing a dwelling, and often be feared in close contact.

You will find that Americans of all colors carry great tension over skin color. In its most destructive form, the tension explodes in an all-consuming bitterness toward others: hate. CAUTION: Hate is contagious. Allowed to run its course, it could sicken and kill you, or drive you to harm others. In your natural desire as a Venusian to be embraced — and your distress at being inexplicably spurned — you may be tempted to hate as well. Do not succumb. Instead, follow these three crucial directives to maintain emotional balance:

1. Immunize yourself.

In America you will witness skin hate everywhere, even in places you would least expect to find it. You will be shocked. Thousands of crimes of racial hate are reported nationally each year, and many more go unreported. Hate organizations are active in all fifty regions of the nation. Hatred is expressed among all skin colors but appears to be keenest between the very light-skinned descendants of enslavers (immigrants from a continent known as Europe who are commonly referred to as "white") and the very dark-skinned descendants of the previously mentioned African slaves, commonly called "black." The hateful behaviors vary: people are attacked and killed, sometimes even castrated and hanged by the neck; places of worship burned; property defaced; telephone threats made; anger expressed in broadcast messages; customers refused service. Even children are ridiculed or treated with public cruelty due to skin color. Curiously, many Americans will share a home with a creature not of their species, yet refuse to inhabit space near a human of a different skin color.

You will wonder how such socially destructive behavior has survived. One reason is that slavery itself ended only recently, and its effects and attitudes persist. Another is that racism gives many (particularly the less prosperous among the whites) a delusion of power. A "black" family moving into a poor "white" area, for example, may be attacked by whites for "bringing down" the neighborhood. This is clearly senseless; the community's problem is poverty, not race. But feeling superior to blacks helps such whites to deny their own powerlessness.

Similarly, Americans are commonly willing to believe racial myths that an off-worlder can immediately recognize as nonsense. Not long ago in one American city, a white man murdered his female mate and claimed that a fictional black attacker committed the crime. Security forces conducted massive searches of black-occupied areas before the truth was revealed. In another instance a white woman drowned her two children and blamed a nonexistent black lawbreaker for their disappearance. In both cases whites uncritically accepted lies that appealed to popular suspicions about blacks. Some black Americans, for their part, embrace a creation myth in which whites are defined as the evil offspring of a wrongdoer.

This bombardment of skin hate may make you feel vulnerable. Resist. Humans entertain skin hatreds due to feelings of being dominated. They lash out against imagined loss of power or security. If a skin-hater expresses animosity toward you, remember that he feels threatened by your presence, and he wants for you to feel the same way. Your defensiveness serves, for him, as proof that his hostility has found its mark. He defines his image of himself, at least in part, by its relation to you. Do not grant him the same power.

Carefully observe a racist's glare. Your presence endangers, in his eyes, something he deems vital: job, stature, safety, opportunity, fantasized superiority. His inflation of his own racial identity, and his denigration of yours, are attempts to restore lost confidence. Do not allow your self-regard to be wounded (and potentially contaminated) by race hate. Recognize, instead, that your Venusianity remains unshaken while the skin-hater's identity, always in need of reassurance, does not.

Remember: Differences between individual Americans are always far greater than differences between ethnic groups — despite what many Americans themselves believe. In the contemporary United States, even some Venusians have been known to yield to the overwhelming pressure of racial hate. BE WARNED: If you surrender to the impulse to judge individuals by anything other than character, you will reach gravely erroneous conclusions. Such mistakes in threat detection can be costly; they can blind you to a human's actual intentions. Do not put yourself at risk.

2. Relearn self-defense.

What you have come to know on Venus as a normal state of awareness around strangers — a kind of relaxed attention — would be viewed by Americans as utter vulnerability to attack. This requires that you change your idea of self-defense. Americans, accustomed as they are to skin hate and to other fears of harm, believe that being constantly braced for invasion of one's person is normal. They accept low-grade, dormant fear as part of daily life, and they also accept its side effects, including numerous stress-related disorders and occasional violent outbursts by males.

Americans endure this from long habit. While you will find it strange and saddening, you will also discover that some individuals bear the stress better than others. Do not presume all Americans to have lost their capacity for joy and trust; you will deny yourself opportunities for bonding. In seeking camaraderie or friendship, carry yourself with readiness for conflict without being possessed by it. Walk through a shopping arena or ride a group transportation device without displaying the "are-you-looking-at-me" and "who-are-you" glances and gestures that haunt the expressions of many light- and dark-skinned Americans in public places. Resist false prompts for combat. Then (as on Venus), on the rare occasions when you must fight, you will feel free to do so, and justified in your self-defense.

3. Engage.

Skin-haters tend to avoid any personal contact with the resented "other" that might change their beliefs. At their most extreme, they not only dislike those they have targeted but also actively prevent themselves from liking them. They associate only with their "own kind," so that their only contact with the "hated" skins is through physical attack or legal procedure. This enables both groups to hate symbols instead of hating actual humans. The cycle continues with the help of resentment bred by poverty and ongoing racial discrimination.

You will sometimes be frustrated by such obstacles to emotional rapport. Proceed with care. Hostilities in America have progressed to the point where channels of communication taken for granted among Venusians — such as the responsibility to both speak and listen face to face — are avoided by many due to mistrust and fear of bodily harm. An attempt to approach a skin-hater with an offer of civilized dialogue or personal openness can, in the wrong situation, cost you your life. You will no doubt observe, with some consternation, that such a demeanor among skin-haters only increases their own unhappiness. And you will find the resulting state of silent — or occasionally explosive — warfare to be hard to tolerate. You will need an intelligent way to approach such hazardous racial barricades.

The answer is to exercise engagement — to thoughtfully breach others' racial barriers in those situations you judge yourself able to manage. As you encounter racial misinformation or hostility in your everyday affairs of work and pleasure, you will face constant choices about whether, when, how, and with whom to personally engage on these matters. Expect no rules. Look, instead, for choices. Any action may be the right or wrong one.

> • *In a drinking establishment, a man of one race allows himself to be drawn into conversation by an extremely large (and intoxicated) man of another race. The drunken man begins to make ill-advised comments about people of the other man's skin color. The two men begin to argue, softly, then loudly. The smaller man wields the superior insult. The larger man wields the superior punch to the jaw. The smaller man instigates legal proceedings. The*

larger man is convicted of assault and sentenced to picking up garbage in lieu of jail.

• A man is flagrantly denied an apartment on the basis of skin color by the owner of a private dwelling. He has all that he needs to file a lawsuit, including a witness of a different race to whom the landlord offered the apartment the next day. The man telephones the landlord. He tells her his team is poised to sue her, and that it is an open-and-shut case: she would be sure to lose. But, he adds, he has far more important things to do right now than to drag as sorry a creature as she to court. But he wants her to know that she has been caught, and that what she did was wrong. She is flabbergasted. She stammers that she meant no such thing. He tells her he knows better. He tells her she will be watched. He tells her to think about what she did. He tells her to have a nice day.

• A man of a dark race decides to become friendly with members of a white skin-hating organization notorious, among other things, for castrating dark-skinned men and hanging them by the neck. The man has dinner with members of this skin-hating group, talks with them, laughs with them. He does this, he explains to an incredulous newspaper reporter, because he believes in the raw power of dialogue. By popular standards, he is crazy. But, he insists, he and his new friends are *at least creating communication where none existed.*

Ultimately, the decision about how to best respond to skin hate must be yours. REMEMBER: Never fear options. Do not be caged by others' hostility. Be willing not only to confront, not only to defend, but also to engage in a manner that has personal effect. This may sometimes means forcing recognition of a person's own skin hate back into their fiercely guarded space. Refuse to allow skin-haters to block the path of personal engagement. Choose carefully. But never relinquish the power to make choices.

May your journey bring fulfillment and prosperity.

6

Killing the Conversation
on Affirmative Action

ow to ensure, if you're white, that a black American will want to slug you instead of listen to you: Whenever you have the opportunity, suggest that no matter how hard he or she has strived, no matter how heroically his or her predecessors have sweated and bled and sacrificed, no matter how impressive his or her performance, and no matter how wonderful his or her talents or accomplishments, an odor of suspicion will always hover over his or her achievements. Ask questions such as "You went to that school?" or "They gave you that job?" to reinforce the impression that the black person's competence is in need of verification. Suggest to black people that you understand, you really do, why an underqualified person might seize upon affirmative action as a means of getting ahead. Above all, make it clear, through your own behavior, that an African American can expect, however unfairly, to be routinely treated as a charity case and condemned to a lifetime of interrogation.

How to guarantee, if you're black, that a white American will want to turn on you without having heard you: *Remind him or her, whenever possible, that America's whole gruesome racial mess springs from white folks' own barbaric behavior, starting with their slaveowning ancestors and continuing on down the bloody line: their insatiable, mindless, amoral greed; their cruelty; their racist mythology; their Jim Crow laws; and in general their determination to deny black Americans the most basic of rights and opportunities. Flog white people whenever you can for ancestral guilt, for thriving in a nation fattened by the wage-free forced labor of millions of black men, women, and children. And put it loudly in a white person's face that even if affirmative action were retroactively to grant to African Americans the entire monetary net worth of the American South, plus immediate tuition-free admission to any school of their choice, this would still not even begin to compensate black Americans for what is owed them.*

Affirmative action. By this point we all have blood trickling from our ears. As usual in such grudge matches over moral superiority, there are those on both sides who have their jaws locked around portions of the truth. Allowing blacks and whites to tear at one another in this way may be good for the shareholders — while we tussle over ever more scarce job opportunities, the minimum wage quietly stagnates, and government's regulatory role in society vanishes — but the race war is bad for just about everything that most of us value: peace, prosperity, the diminished likelihood of having "nigger" scratched into your car enamel or "white motherfucker" hissed behind your back. Much of today's debate over entitlements, reduced as it is to lobbing slogans from behind barriers, does no one any good. We will progress, and our conversation will be meaningful, only if we consent to hear in each other's complaints what we have heretofore dismissed as narrow-minded ranting.

Let's look at some of the taboos in this affirmative-action debate, and see how we might free ourselves of them.

The central fact to which many pro-affirmative-action blacks (and whites) blind themselves is this: affirmative action carries a price. Some white people in some situations who would otherwise have been hired for particular jobs will not get those jobs. This needn't be because of arbitrary "quotas," a favorite bugaboo of affirmative-action critics. It can simply be a matter of applying standards of fairness where there once were none. If a state has a population that is one-fifth black, and whites have traditionally enjoyed a monopoly on managerial-level government jobs in that state, mandating that 20 percent of these jobs go to blacks is not recklessly or arbitrarily applying a "quota." It is justice. At the same time, there are instances in which using quotas — hiring a temporarily heightened proportion of African Americans to bring racial balance to a roster that has been lily-white for a hundred years — is a reasonable and defensible remedy. And the resulting denial of jobs to a proportion of whites is defensible, too, as a necessary, and long overdue, corrective — a collective reimbursement for opportunities withheld.

But many affirmative-action supporters, cowed by the backpedaling in Washington and in state capitols, are afraid even to touch the issues of justifiable cost and investment. They pretend affirmative action has no cost; that no whites will lose opportunities to blacks; that affirmative action is win-win, with no price to be paid, no moral battle to be fought and won among those whites reluctant to yield ground for the greater good. On the key question of what America is actually willing to pay in order to redress old patterns of racism — the question at the very heart of the matter — many in the pro-affirmative-action crowd take a giant pass. In so doing, they pave the way for opponents to crow triumphantly, "Affirmative action *does* have a cost! And we Americans can't afford it!"

Would it not make a more credible case for

affirmative action, and one better suited to honest dialogue, to acknowledge that Yes, affirmative action has a price, one that Americans can afford and must pay? Would it not yield a better conversation were people who favored affirmative action to first acknowledge the price, and then concentrate on making the case for paying that price, rather than running away from the issue?

Which leads to the key conversation-blocker on the anti-affirmative-action side. What many foes of affirmative action steadfastly refuse to hear is this: affirmative action was never meant to be completely painless for white people. Moreover, given the enduring racial legacy of denied opportunity, white Americans ought to be willing to discuss what sacrifices they are willing to make to repair the damage. For too long the moral reasoning behind affirmative action — the idea that it is simply the right thing to do after centuries of rampant discrimination — has been excluded from the debate. It is time it be put back on the table, time that we made the affirmative-action debate a debate over what is right, not over what is least painful.

To some whites — maybe to you — this is unthinkable. How can a contemporary white American be called to task for wrongs committed by distant ancestors? How can a fair-minded, nonracist white man, someone who would never imagine endorsing slavery, yield a civil service job to a black man who scored two points below him on the exam, purely as a means of offsetting an agency's historic racial discrimination? How can citizens who have never contributed directly to racial injustice be asked to help to right it?

I offer two answers for consideration. One is a simple matter of fact and balance: for every flagrant advantage that a white person imagines is granted to blacks through affirmative action, there are ten granted to whites, invisibly and without fanfare, simply because they are white and therefore not subject to the same degree of scrutiny and suspicion. Absence of discrimination is, because of its very nature, a difficult thing for many whites to appreciate. The fact is, despite whatever hardships and trials they endure, whites are passive beneficiaries of America's most aggressive affirmative-action program: the unofficial one. And they will never know the full extent to which this ghostly but ever-present favoritism has determined their destiny.

The other answer involves precedent. Assisting brethren, in the spirit of shared responsibility, is not a new idea. It is the foundation of social security, health insurance, taxation, and union dues. In any civilized society — the New Deal–era United States, modern Scandinavia, and traditional Native American cultures come to mind — citizens pool resources to help one another out of jams. Moreover, the jam in which black Americans find themselves was brought about not by flood or famine but by concerted human effort. Shouldn't Americans be willing to talk about a concerted effort to solve it?

For what it's worth, I would deep-six affirmative action in a heartbeat if America were to pour jillions of dollars into meaningful urban jobs, thereby providing stability, income, social support, a strong tax base, funding for good schools, and a flood of qualified black graduates to sweep into American industry and academia, filling — in one fell swoop of bad-assed jet-black competency and brilliance — all the gaps in opportunity and accomplishment between the races.

But in the end, we may never agree. My point is, whatever side of this debate you are on, if you expect to continue the conversation you are going to have to move beyond the dogma. If you favor affirmative action, you must be willing to defend its costs in the face of its critics; if you oppose it, you must have a thoughtful answer — or admit to honest indifference — to the moral question of repairing the damage done by slavery's legacy, that centuries-long stacking of the deck against blacks. Fail on either score, and you are unlikely to make new converts.

What makes the conversation so difficult for people on both sides of the issue is its tendency to get so personal. When a white person suggests that a black person wouldn't have been hired without the help of a quota, he strikes at the heart of the other's sense of worth. These are fighting words, and they elicit a fighting response. So many such attacks upon black achievement have now been made that even a general criticism of affirmative action by a white person may be taken by a black person as a direct personal assault ("Oh, so you think we're incompetent"). The discussion never even gets to the more substantive issues. Maybe the warring parties would actually find they agree on the need for remedies. They will never know. They're too busy calling each other paranoid or racist.

In the spirit of nonviolence, I propose five ground rules whites and blacks might follow when talking about affirmative action:

1. Talk about issues, not individuals.

Discussing how well or how badly an individual performs his or her job should be left to formal evaluators — or to gossips. It has no place in an argument about national racial policy. Anyone can come up with convenient examples of workplace idiots or heroes. They come in all sizes and colors, and they are hired for all kinds of reasons. Anchoring your argument in "so-and-so's incompetence" will mire you in an endless battle of petty testimonials, prove nothing, and put everyone on the defensive. Save the personal insinuations for private conversations. In public debates over affirmative action, there is only one question: Are our communities better off with it, or are they better off without it?

2. Don't start off on the defensive.

On a hot-button topic such as affirmative action, the best way to provoke a hostile response is to act as if you expect it. A preamble such as "Don't take this the wrong way" is a dead giveaway to a listener that you're about to say something he will consider offensive. If you're that uneasy about the conversation, no prelude will help. Make a decision to wade in and take your licks, or to hold your tongue and forget about it. If you do speak, don't be terrified of disagreement. Demonstrate through your tone that you are confident of the mutual ability to argue respectfully. A display of confidence in the relationship will help the other person to relax as well — whether they agree with your position or not.

3. Bring up the topic only when it is relevant.

Few things are more patronizing, especially to a black person, than being asked out of the blue, "So, what do you think of affirmative action?" — as if being a member of a minority makes one an automatic expert on, or a spokesman for, that minority (see chapter 13). Knowing that person very well is a different story; friendship has its own rules. Otherwise, approach affirmative action as you would any other controversial issue: bring it up when it seems appropriate, and in a setting conducive to honest conversation. The office hallway is a bad place. A corner table at a café is a good place.

4. If you don't want to be stereotyped, don't buy stereotypes.

Stereotypes kill dialogues quicker than any other toxin. With regard to affirmative action, the classic white mistake is to make sweeping judgments about minority competence. Throughout my adult life, when I have mentioned to people that I graduated from Harvard, more often than not the news has been greeted with raised eyebrows. "*You* went to Harvard?" I have learned to come back with quick replies — such as, "Yes, why do you ask?" — that stop people in their tracks. I have no doubt that I fit Harvard's affirmative-action guidelines. I also have no doubt that I belonged there. What I find interesting, however — and what I found true at Harvard — is that many of the whites who seem incredulous about my achievements come from well-off families with their own long tradition of "affirmative action" — in the form of legacy admissions to schools their parents attended, jobs for one another's kids, and political contacts.

The premise of affirmative action — that rules can be bent for the sake of diversity without ill effect — is subject to debate. But the fact of human individuality should not be. Don't confuse the two by presuming minorities to be unqualified. You will end up sounding less than intelligent yourself.

The classic conversation-killer, on the part of a black person, is to smear a white person with a thick coat of blame for slavery, and to presume, moreover, that all whites need to be lectured on the subject of culpability. Whether because of ignorance or denial, some whites do lack an understanding of slavery's profound significance. (So do many blacks, for that matter.) But casting whites as enemies, and personalizing the hostility with a tone of "this is what you did to us," only fuels white defensiveness. They know, whether they admit it or not, that their ancestors did something horribly wrong. They also know that it happened before they were born. To treat white people as passive stewards of racism who need to be force-fed remedies is to ignore the real inner conflict many of them already feel — and to shut down the potential good that inner conflict can bring, whether in confronting hard truths about affirmative action or some other issue. If you're going to sabotage the process, why even talk?

5. Don't assume who is "for" and who is "against."

We all know, but still need to remind ourselves, that opinions about affirmative action do not follow strictly racial lines. There are blacks — as well as members of other minority groups — who question or even oppose affirmative action. There are whites who champion it. If you bet on being able to anticipate "what *they* think," you may lose.

There are no short cuts. If you really want to end by understanding, learn how to start the conversation.

7

Elvis Has *Not* Left the Building

[Elvis] was the first person in America to get a hysterical white mob to approach a black phenomenon without violating the Bill of Rights.

— Mark Crispin Miller

Before the chins, before the shovel-sized belt buckles and the carpeted Graceland ceilings, before even the possibility of my-life-with-Elvis paperbacks or the occasional K-Mart sightings, there was just a quiet, skinny white kid from Tupelo, Mississippi, with bad acne and a bone-deep love of music. Any music: rhythm and blues, hymnal, hillbilly. He didn't set out to become anybody's symbol of sex or race or gluttony or velvet immortality. His goals were more basic: to raise his tenor tremolo to the rafters, like the r&b and gospel artists whom he admired; to convulse for screaming girls like a loosely clothed jackhammer; and to drive a pink Cadillac.

Look at poor Elvis today: a hollow sideburned monstrosity mocked, mimicked, and merchandised as the patron saint of kitsch; preserved in as many incarnations as there are varieties of plastic; enthroned as an idol by a throng for whom teenage hipness calcified somewhere between Pat Boone and James Brown; embraced worldwide as a handy metaphor for any given American excess, whether randy brashness, dull-wittedness, or overeating; revered as "the King"; reviled by many African Americans as a strutting symbol of white exploitation of black music; subject to more eye-rolling among blacks than anyone this side of Al Jolson.

The real racial rub about Elvis stems not from any lack of talent — he had it coming out of his pores — nor from the aura of trailer-park white tackiness that clings to him, but from the simple fact of his having taken a black form — in this case, the black dance music popular on segregated "race records" of the 1940s and 1950s — and made it suddenly and lucratively marketable to the white mainstream. Ask black Americans what they think of Elvis, or any other white credited with the "birth of rock and roll," such as Bill Haley and the Comets, and they'll tell you that it's the same old plantation gig all over again: black labor, white profit.

When it comes to Elvis at least, this may be

somewhat of a cheap shot. For one thing, Elvis brilliantly and intuitively spanned the distance between the black urban and white rural musical vernaculars. And he was hardly the first, or the last, white figure to benefit from doing the black thing. We know, for instance, that black music has served as the bedrock for American popular music itself, as Amiri Baraka (LeRoi Jones), Dominique-René de Lerma, Eileen Southern, Phyl Garland, David Baker, and many other music historians have long since shown. Moreover, outrageous racial copycatting cuts both ways: look at Michael Jackson's surgically remodeled nose. But that's another story.

So why pick on Elvis? Because he provides such an obvious meeting place. Because his famed pelvis was quite literally the modern pivot point, the commercial bone-and-socket at which our jangling black and white limbs are connected. Elvis is where Johnnie Ray meets Madonna, and where Bob Dylan meets Fats Domino. Elvis is where a white girl in Cleveland dances with a black boy in Jim Crow Alabama. Elvis is where miscegenation in American music officially went big-time. Deny Elvis, and you deny the very fact of black and white American dancers being joined at the hip.

Before our next dance-hall rumble over cultural ownership of the megachains' entire stock of pop CDs, let's settle this thing. When you get beyond his bad taste and bad behavior, the ontological debate (Elvis as King versus Elvis as Prince of Thieves) really comes down to whether what he bequeathed to fans was his to bequeath. As usual, there is a whole lot of denyin' going on. On both sides. Closure in mixed company will come only, I think, when we all digest two essential facts:

Fact One: Elvis repackaged a black product for the white market. At a huge profit.

Ain't no disputin' it. Although black music was hardly Elvis's only influence — he listened to and absorbed everything from backwoods folk to country gospel to city blues, as Peter Guralnick has most recently made clear in his exhaustive Elvis biography, *Last Train to Memphis* — black r&b lay at the heart of his recording career. Sun Records founder Sam Phillips, the first to record Elvis, made no bones about it:

> [Black] records appealed to white youngsters just as Uncle Silas [Payne's] songs and stories used to appeal to me. . . . But there was something in many of those youngsters that resisted buying this music. . . . They liked the music, but they weren't sure whether they ought to like it or not. So I got to thinking how many records you could sell if you could find white performers who could play and sing in this same exciting, alive way.

What Phillips recognized as the breakthrough in Elvis's early studio sessions came when, after fruitless hours of doodling with ballads, Elvis broke spontaneously into a rendition of black r&b artist Arthur "Big Boy" Crudup's "That's All Right (Mama)." Phillips sat up straight. Tape rolled. The rest was history: Elvis's string of five consecutive hits for Sun in 1954 and 1955, including Wynonie Harris's "Good Rockin' Tonight" and Little Junior Parker and the Blue Flames' "Mystery Train." All were either covers of r&b tunes or country songs sung in r&b style.

That's why, when his voice was first launched over the airwaves throughout the unsuspecting American South, Elvis Aron Presley sounded black. Very black. So black, in fact, that his first radio interviewer, in Memphis, made it a point to have Elvis mention to listeners that he had attended (segregated) Humes High School. As the interviewer later explained to a writer, "I wanted to get that out, because a lot of people listening had thought he was colored."

But there was more to Elvis's cultural novelty than sounding black. In *Boxed In: The Culture of TV*, media critic Mark Crispin Miller goes further: "Elvis' appropriation of blackness was not restricted to his music. . . . [L]ike Brando, he did not look entirely white (a statement that might have annoyed him), but seemed a curious amalgam of the races: with his full lips, broad nose, and jet-black hair (dyed), he was a new kind of idol, looking ahead to such Sixties celebrities as Mick Jagger and Malcolm McDowell."

Provocative, but true. As physical specimen, Elvis was an entirely new cut of white pop hero, a bad boy somewhere out on the edges of whiteness. Even his face announced it. He was an ad agency's crossover dream. Not that he was any Machiavellian master of Jim Crow strategic marketing. Even his most sympathetic biographers stop well short of granting him that kind of visionary acumen, although his handlers knew exactly what they had and how to promote it. But Elvis himself was basically a white kid from off the main roads who knew what music he liked, and who played and sang and kept stubbornly showing up at the offices of Sun Records, month after month, until he finally got his break. Above all, he was the right performer with the right stuff at the right time for a postwar white generation bored with conformity, popping with sexual desire, and intrigued by (but legally estranged from) most of black culture.

Elvis — the young Elvis, the thin Elvis — went into the studio and got crazy. He didn't map out a scheme to go crazy; he just *went crazy*, honky-tonk crazy, with the music he had always loved, and on the air and in the record stores a certain dark craziness suddenly became permissible, accessible to hordes of young white listeners. And then Elvis went to Hollywood, and the Chords and Big Joe Turner and Wynonie Harris and LaVern Baker and Little Richard and the scores of other black pioneers of the dark craziness who saw their own songs rerecorded as smash hits by white artists were left behind (often with no copyright protection) to make chump change. It ain't pretty. But it's history.

Fact Two: Elvis was a great artist.

Elvis was baaad. As in good. As in insurgent and innovative and willing to be weird. As in brilliantly creative in the particular crossover chemistry that he brought to pop music.

Here is what makes dissing Elvis a dicey enterprise: even as he raided the r&b catalog and moved in the shadows of black dance music, he made forays of his own in the musical lexicon that are astonishing and enduring — as a singer, a performer, a musical superhero. I mean, that machine-gun leg movement, cranking epileptically in the billowing fabric behind his knife-edged pant crease as if he were being rhythmically peeled to the bone. And the patented pelvis, not just suggestively undulating in the familiar honky-tonk way but childishly herky-jerky, grinding out a message of salvation for the repressed teenage victims of the white puritanical tradition. And his voice, poised between stab and sob. And that perfectly ugly sneer, its weepy threat of babylike violence complemented by his downturned lips and eyes. This was no mere lip-synching of race records. This was all

Elvis. This was synapse and spirit, a man moving with his eyes closed. The kind of thing you might well expect from a kid who, as Elvis's adolescent friends unanimously seem to recall, was always — in his manner and in his dress — kind of strange.

All this made up the man who came gyrating across the bridge to the white territories: not just a black-sounding singer who (hot damn!) turned out to be a white fella, but one who also opened a whole new theater of possibilities, in which hillbilly twang had a backbeat and an uptown attitude; in which being mean-assed was cool; in which white girls were allowed to scream; in which sex among white teenagers at last found expression; in which sneering violence became musical eroticism; in which whites could dance with blacks without crossing the tracks. Look out across any ocean-sized arena today in which thousands of white kids roar at costumed performers ripping through amplified variations on the blues, and you can pretty well say, "Elvis was here."

If you are white, you might fairly well accept the notion of Elvis as the conquering lion (or hippo) of pop. If you are black, you may glower in the face of the King. What are we supposed to do with Elvis, who is still among us raising hell? It is tempting to call him a thief, even while pointing to him as evidence that white musicians can get down, too. To the extent that African Americans spitefully deny Elvis even the least amount of legitimacy, they fail to appreciate what he *did* bring to the party. And to the extent that whites deny what Elvis "borrowed" from black musical sources on his way to the prom, they become accomplices to a cultural lie.

The answer is for blacks and whites to come to some kind of mutual acknowledgment of Elvis. I'm not suggesting we need town meetings on Elvis. Just truthful confrontation. Have you noticed that white people rarely bring up the subject of Elvis in racially mixed company? Or that black people almost never mention Elvis as being among their formative adolescent influences? When blacks and whites mix, they maneuver around Elvis, without comment, as if he were an elephant in our living room. When the blacks leave the room, whites dance with the elephant; when the whites leave, blacks laugh at it. It's all very dysfunctional.

The search for closure on Elvis is simultaneously absurd and inevitable. Imagine community leaders and talk show hosts beseeching white and black Americans to talk about Elvis across racial lines. On the other hand, imagine blacks and whites trying to embrace any sort of shared experience of post-World War Two American pop music without addressing him. There is no way around it. Praise him, curse him, call him royalty, call him sewer scum. But call him ours. And acknowledge that at some level we all dance to much of the same music.

In the end, the Elvis story is really about myths of creation. I can imagine some cosmic authority finally stepping in to mete out judgment on our cultic conflict over Elvis:

HEAR ME, *white rock and rollers. I command you to stop believing that Elvis appeared one day out of nowhere. I order you to nod to your black brethren for their role in creating Elvis, and that, further, you begin cutting large royalty checks to key black musicians, beginning with the heirs of blues great Robert Johnson. . . .*

AND HEAR ME, *African-American Elvis-bashers. I order you to stop pretending that Elvis was a talentless, feckless imposter with no gift of his own. And even while I decree justice — and overdue royalties — for black music, I insist that you give artistic credit where it is due, whether to Elvis or to anyone else.*

In the meantime, it comes down to us mortals, face to face on the dance floor. So tell me: what do you think of the music?

Identity

8

Black? African American? European American? White? What's in Our Names?

*I*t has been said of the Jews that they became white only upon arrival in America. Richard Pryor used to do a stand-up routine in which he described newly arrived immigrants at Ellis Island being drilled on how to properly pronounce the preferred American term for black people: "Nigger! . . . Nigger! . . . Nigger! . . . Nigger!"

One might argue that whiteness was invented in America; it appeared as a suddenly compulsory trait among the landowning classes at roughly the same time that manacled blue-black Africans began *descending ramps from ships. Skin color, along with the theories springing from it, has remained our national preoccupation ever since. So it is no surprise that as a nation, we have spun through a good half-dozen names for blackness and a growing list for whiteness in the space of the past century alone.*

Okay. But what makes black *preferable to* Negro, *and* Negro *preferable to* colored, *and* African American *preferable to all of them? Who decides between* Caucasian, white, *and now* European American? *Is there a logic behind this evolution of forms of address, and can we put it to good use in an attempt to understand one another? Or, as the Paleolithic down-with-diversity crowd likes to mutter, are we surrendering our wits to an orgy of linguistic glad-handing?*

Never, ever, let anyone talk you into believing that names, in the skinfest that we call American cultural consciousness, do not matter. They do. Moreover, our long and ragged process of racial self-appellation has its own compelling logic. From the black side, beginning with *colored* and ending with *African American*, names for Americans of African descent have grown increasingly specific in acknowledging our origins. It is no coincidence that this has been accompanied by a deepening pride in African heritage and in transatlantic family lineage. For a people brought here forcibly as slaves and labeled for centuries as being without history, the embrace of connections with our past is vital to defining who we have become.

To some, especially to whites, such emphasis on the significance of names may seem strange. Why should it make such a difference? Taken by themselves, *colored* and *Negro* are fairly bland terms that, emptied of historical associations, might arguably be as good as any other. But names are more than letters and sounds. They signify much more than mere physical description. To many black people, *colored* and *Negro* are mired in Jim Crow America, when segregation was accepted as law and lynchings were weekend blood sport for crowds of white families. *Colored* and *Negro* (or its purposely derogatory southern white vernacular version, *Nigra*) became, in their very sounds, sharp signifiers of flagrant racial hatred — labels chosen and uttered with malice by whites. The rise of the term *African American* represents an act of self-definition — a reclaiming of personal legacy by black people in this country. In that sense, if you are white, the choice of names for black people is not yours to make or to judge. Even if you do not understand it, respect it.

As to the mechanics of usage: for Americans of African descent, *African American* is appropriate in all situations, and is now preferred. *Black* is also generally accepted as shorthand, and is often (as in this book) used interchangeably with *African American*. (Remember, though, that *black* is a broader category than *African American*; a black citizen of Ghana or Italy is *not* an African American.) Some people capitalize the first letter of *black*, believing that this constitutes a stronger statement of identity. Others, like me, believe that *black* and *white*, not being used as proper nouns (not references to specific peoples or places), should not be capitalized. This is a matter of preference and, sometimes, debate. There are some African Americans who take offense at lowercase *black* but accept it when capitalized. There are others who take offense at anything other than *African American*. Most, however, will not get riled over the use of either term. I prefer *African American*, but I also consider *black* acceptable; using both, particularly when writing, can help to cut down on repetition, as when a Mexican American also uses *Chicano*.

In its period of greatest popularity (the 1960s and 1970s), *Afro-American* was a significant step forward in acknowledging links to Africa. Its ongoing use in academic settings (e.g., Afro-American studies departments) still lends it some legitimacy. But to my mind the phrase has always seemed a poor compromise (what is "Afro"? Some vague not-quite-African past?), and it has now been generally eclipsed. Better to avoid it. As for *Negro* and *colored*, both have long since fallen from favor. Avoid them. Even people who grew up calling themselves *Negro* or *colored* are, with few exceptions, no longer comfortable with these terms, and anyone who came of age in the 1960s or later is almost certain to take offense. (Note, however, that *people of color* is a widely used and accepted phrase in reference to all peoples of non-European descent.) As for addressing those few who stubbornly prefer *colored* or *Negro* to anything else — you're going to have to offend somebody. Choose.

For some white Americans, *European American* has recently emerged as an alternative term for white, although it has gained nothing approaching the popularity of *African American*. Most whites simply do not feel the need for a term that explicitly links them to Europe. Given the overwhelming manner in which those of European ancestry have dominated official American history, practically all who hear the term *white* will implicitly make the European connection. Contrast this with the experience of African Americans, who have long hungered to break the silence (and dispel the misrepresentations) shrouding their past. Among whites who feel an analogous hunger to anchor themselves in European tradition (the more zealous amateur genealogists of European family lineage come to mind, as do, in the extreme case, certain white supremacists), *European American* has a powerful appeal.

I see *European American* as a discretionary term that is interchangeable with *white* most of the time. If you are white and feel that *European American* best describes you, use it; if it matters enough to you, make your preference known to others. It is reasonable, I think, for a person with such feelings to ask friends and acquaintances to refer to him or her as a *European American*. It is going too far, though, to expect a universal preference for *European American* in the way that *African American* is preferred by blacks.

As I said, with American culture having for so long celebrated its European roots and ignored (or vilified) its African ones, black Americans have experienced an erosion of basic identity that most white Americans have not. In our nation's notion of its history, Europe is central and Africa peripheral or invisible. As I've heard many blacks quip over America's lack of a designated month for white history: "*Every month is white history month.*"

There may be instances in which white persons of non-European ancestry (white immigrants from Australia or Brazil, for example) choose a specific term (*Australian American, Brazilian American*) rather than the catchall *white*. Again, others should honor such persons' wishes; it seems to me that both the specific and general terms are appropriate, depending upon how closely the person identifies with his country of origin. If you are black, respect a white person's choice in this matter as you would expect them to respect your own.

There is often a difference between how people refer to themselves and how they expect to be referred to by others. Particularly within historically oppressed groups of Americans, such self-appellation can serve to strengthen a sense of unity, a feeling that some experience is "just between us." There are, for example, few cryptic synonyms for whiteness that are meant to be understood only by American Caucasians. On the other hand, there are many such self-defining terms among Jews, peoples of color, and other groups whose history has made them feel out-side of the mainstream. Among blacks, calling one another "brother" and "sister" is a symbolic way of saying, "We are in this together." To refer to a third party as a brother or a sister is shorthand for saying that he or she is black and therefore shares a certain understanding. Despite having been appropriated by countless synthetic hipsters of all races, it is a form of self-address that retains its potency.

Today, some progressive black leaders make it a point to refer to *any* person of goodwill, whatever his or her race, as a brother or a sister, the implicit mes-sage being that justice transcends skin color. But in casual use, the terms tend to be reserved for blacks and for those few whites who are accepted as cultur-ally "black." Other whites who fling around such terms in black company will likely find the reception chilly.

I once learned what it feels like to commit such a gaffe. I was having a conversation with a Native American woman who casually referred to herself as a "'skin." The way she used the word sounded cool to me, and, without thinking, I used "'skin" to refer to myself as a person of color. I was immediately and emphatically reprimanded; the term, she said, was a derivative of *redskin* and was to be used *by Native Americans only*. Perhaps she expressed the feeling of most Native Americans; perhaps not. All the same, the lesson is that "just-between-us" speech can be closely guarded, and its rules cannot be taken for granted. If you do not know the language well, don't try to speak it.

This brings us to that thermonuclear implement of insider (and outsider) slang, *nigger*. Among black Americans, there is a long history of using *nigger,* both as an insult (sometimes playfully) and as a defiant display of self-contempt. I remember as a child trading spirited accusations of "Nigger!" — along with the occasional dirt clod — with other children in the black neighborhood where my family lived until I was eight. Ours was the same mixed message as that of many black children who fling the word at one another today: on one level, we were appropriating a potent word for our own use in an age-old game of verbal gotcha. Just beneath, though, we were telling ourselves, "I am a nigger. I am somewhat less than white. And I would rather call myself and my friends niggers than wait for white people to call us niggers."

To make any pronouncement about how people should and should not refer to themselves is inherently risky. Such judgment implies an ability to read people's minds, to understand what they *mean* when they embrace a certain word. There is no way for anyone to assess the self-esteem of every black person who calls someone a nigger, just as it is impossible to diagnose self-hatred in every gay man who playfully calls another a faggot. People juggle knives when they play with their own stereotypes. Whether they emerge lacerated or unscathed has to do with much more than their vocabulary. I know some African Ameri-

cans who decry any use of *nigger* by black people —
but who then turn around and display classic symp-
toms of self-hatred, such as referring to straight,
Caucasian-type hair as "good hair." I also know
supremely confident, racially proud African Americans who nonetheless occasionally kid one another in
private with the term *nigger*.

It is hard to imagine any reasoned justification
for blacks to use *nigger* — a word born of racism —
in self-reference. I have yet to hear anyone make a co-
gent argument in its defense. I believe that black
children should be told of the epithet's wicked history
and taught not to use it. But those (such as I) who disapprove of the word must also beware of our own
tendency to stereotype all blacks who use it. Whether
we like it or not, playful use of *nigger* can, like telling
"black" jokes (which I'll discuss later) fall into the
category of things that self-respecting black adults
feel they oughtn't do but sometimes do anyway. The
only way to knowledgeably judge a person is by
knowing him.

There is, however, another black use of *nigger*
that is not at all ambivalent. Its mega-strength distil-
lation emerged in the 1980s with the use of *nigga* vir-
tually as a mantra in the most violent gangsta rap.
For such eighties rappers as NWA (Niggaz with Attitude) and the early Ice-T, being a nigga meant being
the ultimate outlaw, being an armed desperado with
the power to destroy oneself before white society
could do the job. It meant invulnerability through

101

suicide. It proved to be an irresistible image for both alienated young would-be black gangstas who sought power through guns and money, and alienated white suburban kids who sought bunk-bed rebellion. It also proved colossally profitable for the recording industry, which, despite concessions to pressure from political and religious groups, has continued to sell this image of the young black male identity in a variety of forms.

This defiant use of *nigger* as self-reference captures, more than any other act, the desperate dilemma of black identity: self-hatred coupled with a stubborn resolve for self-determination. To proclaim oneself a nigger is to declare to the disapproving mainstream, "You can't fire me. I quit." Hence the perennial popularity of the word among poor black youth who at the same time carry a burning resentment of white society. To growl that one is a nigga is a seductive gesture of self-caricature — and one that can feel bitterly empowering. It may be as inherently destructive as any white bigot using *coon, jungle bunny, moolie,* and all the rest. But again, even if you disapprove of a young black person using the word, look more deeply before branding his heart. Increasingly, we are pushing many young black males to view angry self-sacrifice as the only remaining path to personal power.

At the risk of stating the obvious, I will emphasize here that I have been talking strictly about the use of the word *by blacks*. If you are white, it is much simpler: use of *nigger* is completely off-limits, unless you happen to be one of the few whites so deeply assimilated into black life that it is not an issue. If you have to ask yourself whether using *nigger* is okay, it is not. An African American who cries nigger is playing with fire, but it is his own property — his identity — that he places at risk. A white American who cries nigger is lighting a blaze in someone else's house — and will likely be treated as an arsonist.

There are as many ugly synonyms for whiteness as there are for blackness, and you have probably heard them all: *honky, ofay, snow girl, punk,* and so on. The same principles of decorum and self-respect apply here as well. One significant difference, though, is that through the sheer weight of white racism in our society, antiblack epithets carry much more destructive firepower than antiwhite ones. Or, put another way, a much higher proportion of blacks call themselves niggers than whites call themselves honkies. The effect is that while the collective black psyche is strafed by artillery fire, the white psyche fends off an occasional BB pellet.

As I've said, this imbalance holds true for the entire racist exchange between blacks and whites in America. It does not, however, change the essential rules of decent human conduct: calling people names is wrong. Don't do it. And if you call yourself names, start asking yourself why.

9

Congratulations! You're Ethnic!

My nearest dictionary to hand defines ethnic as "1. Heathen; pagan; pertaining to nations or groups neither Christian nor Jewish. 2. Designating or of any of the basic divisions or groups of mankind, as distinguished by customs, characteristics, language, etc."

Right off, there's a conflict: by old-fashioned standards of white ethnocentrism (as in the first definition above), only swarthy non–Western Europeans — that majority of the world's population seen as exotic "others" — rate the label of "ethnic." But by modern standards (as in the second definition), everybody is ethnic: you, me, even Beaver Cleaver. This sows terrible confusion among crowds at Disney World. What *constitutes cultural normalcy? Do we stick with the fabled ethnic folklore of European conquest, with Yul Brynner as the wild-eyed King of Siam and Deborah Kerr as the civilized soul who tames him? Or do we embrace the more recent definitions in our dictionaries, updated with the help of immigration and sit-ins?*

Crossed signals fly everywhere. At the megasupermarket in my neighborhood, you'll find kente-patterned bandages in the first-aid section, and smiling black faces pictured among the greeting cards. Meanwhile, all of the black hair products are still to be found crammed beneath a sign marked "ethnic," while presumably nonethnic hair goo for Caucasians goes by such placidly universal shelf signage as "shampoos" and "dyes." Our schools preach a singsong "diversity" gospel ("we're all weird and we're all normal") almost to the point of genuflection. Yet in a popular guide to university scholarships, I stumbled across a fund for minority students with the stated purpose of providing "financial assistance to students of ethnic origin." And when American academics refer to "ethnic" or "cultural" studies, they generally mean brown- or red- or yellow-bannered encampments, not those astonishingly European-focused camps demurely labeled as "History" or "Languages."

You could call all of this just more soul-on-your-sleeve multicultural carping. After all, why should we care how things are labeled as long as we can find them in supermarkets and in classrooms?

I'll tell you why. Because when you buy into the peripheral ethnicity of nonwhites, and the central nonethnicity of whites, whether with supermarket products or college curricula, you buy into a massive lie. Like astronomers before Galileo, you entertain a false idea of what (or who) resides at the center of all things. Like anyone with a bad map, sooner or later — in these increasingly nonwhite environs — you are not going to know where you are.

Many Americans — of all races — suffer from the delusion that ethnicity is a characteristic limited to people of color, an odd sort of cultural texturing that whites and their traditions are presumed to lack. Looked at this way, ethnicity becomes a subtle but indelible scarlet letter of nonwhiteness, a marker dye separating that which is familiar from that which is, well, *different*. It becomes a way of placing white culture, in particular, in a category apart from all others, a way of exempting whiteness from any sense of cultural relativism, and therefore of keeping white culture firmly at the center of approved American reality — while the perceived "ethnic" cultures whirl about as orbiting social satellites. By this definition, the sound of salsa music blaring from an apartment window and the wafting aroma of a black chicken-and-ribs restaurant are both "ethnic," while the munching of a tuna sandwich on white bread by a white Anglo-Saxon man in green pants is, hysterically enough, "normal." My point is that, increasingly, we are all coming to recognize that white Americans are ethnic, too.

I mean, how much more ethnic can you get than hair that falls limply in any direction instead of kinkily holding its own? What could be more ethnic a trait than sunburn? Or than wearing shorts in winter? Or — here's a bizarre one for you — than insisting that music be written down and performed by rote (rather than composed in spontaneous reverie) in order to qualify as a serious effort of the human heart and intellect? For that matter, how much more strange could any culture be than the technology-intoxicated, increasingly dispirited society in which we now live? How can anyone, anywhere, make any pretenses to nonethnicity or cultural inertness?

Getting suckered into believing in the nutty idea of cultural centrality will damage people more than they know. To give just one example, obstinate white huddling around inherited European forms is why, tragically, America ranks somewhere near last in the world — certainly well behind Japan and all of Europe — in appreciating the significance of jazz. And by jazz I do not mean Tommy Dorsey or Najee or Kenny G. I mean men and women, mostly but not exclusively African American, schooled in the merciless crucible of public musical improvisation, in which gemlike technical mastery is expected and instant fluency in all keys of one's soul is demanded. Every night. In front of strangers.

You'll notice that I'm not talking about whether or not Americans *like* jazz. I'm talking about whether or not they recognize its stature, in the way that, say, a woman who has never once listened to Beethoven will reflexively utter his name when her third-grade son asks her to name a "great" musician for his school assignment. Her confidence that Beethoven is central to music has nothing to do with liking or even knowing his art. His importance is one of a thousand cultural facts that she memorized at an early age. She hasn't the least bit of feeling for his music's heart-bursting intensity. But she knows that he matters. A lot.

In the same way, you can dislike or even hate jazz and still give it its due as one of the most significant forms of artistic expression of this century. It is easily the harmonic and rhythmic equal (if not better) of any of the world's most sophisticated musical forms, including those by the more difficult European composers. And heart? Listen to Charlie "Bird" Parker, blowing those genius worm-trains of Swiss watch–synchronized chords at warp speed, each chosen, impossibly, with angelically lyrical foreknowledge. There is Miles Davis, creating, literally, his own language of tight-throated, galaxy-spaced tonal travel. There is Billie Holiday, making of the human voice a flared horn. There is John Coltrane, reincarnating Western scales and Eastern modes in hurricane prayer spasms that reduce the thronged faithful in New York basement nightclubs to howls and shivers.

But, as I said, you might hate jazz. There are plenty of people in Tokyo and Paris who do. Even a French or Japanese jazz hater, though, is far likelier than an American to acknowledge the music's importance, its place in the world of serious music. Ask any jazz musician how he or she is received in Europe, Asia, or Africa as compared with America, and he or she will tell you how Americans undervalue jazz. Joachim Berendt, to name one scholar among scads of them, calls jazz "America's most autonomous and important contribution to world culture." He is German. (His much-reprinted *The Jazz Book,* by the way, is a must-read on black American music, as is Amiri Baraka's *Blues People.*) The first published study of jazz by a white person was written by a Swiss conductor named Ernest Ansermet in 1919. The first book on jazz was written by a Belgian, Robert Goffin, in 1929. The first jazz magazine was edited by a Frenchman, Hugues Panassie, beginning in the late 1920s. They all knew that this American music had changed the world.

Americans should know this, too. In the same way that those of us only slightly familiar with music are willing to grant the greatness of classical music, we should know the equally monumental global stature of jazz. We could enlarge our pantheon of officially sanctioned and supported mainstream creative heroes — as opposed to the marginal "great hip genius" stature generally reserved for jazz immortals — to include Louis as well as Ludwig, Miles as well as

Mozart. Were it not for American white ethnocentric inertia, we might. But many of us are not listening for even the waves made by jazz. In the supermarket of our national culture, jazz is relegated to the ethnic aisle. And our dominant idea of shampoo is the culturally "normal" kind — an aisle away.

Let me be clear: there are musical forms in America more marginalized than jazz, and they are not all black. The list includes bluegrass, zydeco, cajun, salsa, blues, and numerous others. Many are treated with greater respect abroad than here. Even blues, revered as it is by many of the rock-and-roll generation, has missed out on much of the fame and fortune of the commercial music it helped to inspire. Moreover, some marginalization — say, not being appreciated by the young — is common to practically all classic art forms, jazz included.

But no American art form, in any field, has been as venerated worldwide — as established and canonized — as jazz. It is this very global veneration that makes its diminished stature in America — its being viewed more as entertainment than as art — so striking. It is a unique predicament that is hard to explain on any other basis than cultural bias. Having been pedigreed by so many scholars and musicians over the past century as being at the very heart of American life, jazz provides a classic example of the power of white American denial.

What you and I must realize is simply that we are all, every one of us, as gratingly ethnic in our manners and habits as my loudest and brassiest relative; we are all as improbable and as inexplicable as the young black kids who gyrate miraculously to their own beats, or the Zen poet sheep rancher I met in Wyoming; we are all as odd as gefilte fish or white bread or American cheese or roasted tapir; we are as enigmatic as voodoo and sacrificed chickens and acupressure and the sweat-lodge ceremony.

Being ethnic means being alive. Each of us, no matter how serene our notion of normalcy, is as bizarre and unbelievable an ethnic creation as the world has ever seen. And we are surrounded by approximately 6 billion people who know it. Our national game of bland non-ness, of objective centrality, is lost; give it up. As you go through whatever social motions you might find familiar — applying suntan lotion, teaching about the Pilgrims, spreading blue cheese on expensive crackers, doing an Elvis imitation, combing your hair — remind yourself: *this is ethnic.* Begin to consider your characteristics, and your habits, as no less strange than those of, say, your immigrant neighbors who cook that funny-smelling food. Which is to say, understand that those neighbors view you the same way.

And while you're at it, stop buying into the ethnic labeling in supermarkets. In fact, if you own a store, change your signs. If you need a sign highlighting black hair products, what's wrong with "African American"? Okay, maybe it's a hassle referring to groups by name. But are you unwilling to expend a few extra minutes, or a few extra cents, to do the right thing for your customers?

For a sharpened sense of what it means to share the world, consider picking up a copy of *The Dictionary of Global Culture,* edited by Kwame Anthony Appiah and Henry Louis Gates, Jr. From Arabic literature to traditional Japanese clothing, from American presidents to Lebanese poets, it's an alphabetically ordered reminder of the vastness of everything we call *culture.* Leaf through it once and you'll never feel nonethnic again.

We may all find that being ethnic is not so bad. For one thing, it makes for great listening.

10

"Hey, Yo!": Black Talk, White Talk, and the Color of Speech

Take this quiz:

1. A young black male customer wearing non-descript clothing approaches the counter in a store. The cashier is white. How is the cashier likely to address the black customer, about whom he knows nothing?

___ "Yo, help you, my man?"

___ "May I help you?"

2. A female black attorney takes a cold call from a potential client, who is white. She so impresses the client that he wants to come in and meet with her right away. At the appointed time, the client

walks into the attorney's office and sees that she is black. How is he likely to react?

__ Display his shock

__ Hide his shock

__ Consider her race unworthy of note

3. Young people speak "black English" because:

__ Schools can barely stay afloat, let alone offer instruction in elocution

__ Their families and friends speak it

__ They think standard English is for bookish punks

__ They are white, suburban, and trying to be cool

The correct answers? Well, for better or for worse, all of the above are "correct" in the sense that they reflect what actually happens, or they explain things that you and I face every day. And they tell us something essential: speech is a high-stakes ethnic code, a set of clues we use to make instant decisions about strangers.

We screen each others' language like soldiers on patrol in a combat zone, or a scouting party from the starship *Enterprise*. You see a youngish black man in a store? You make him, in your mind's eye, walk the walk and talk the talk, even if he is a medical student from Shaker Heights. You talk to someone on the phone who speaks Standard English? She's white. It's automatic. Her being black does not even appear on the radar screen of possibilities; mastering the language of mainstream achievement is a white thing, right? Black kids whose schools have no textbooks learn that lesson early.

Language is loaded. Speaking Standard English as I do, I regularly get taken for white on the telephone — a wild contrast to the way in which I am commonly taken for a yo in person. In my days as a newspaper reporter, I found my perceived dual identity to be alternately useful and funny. I once telephoned a black editor at an African-American newspaper about doing a freelance story for them, and he declared proudly that his publication would be "happy to consider a white writer." Every black Standard English speaker has stories of making business arrangements on the phone and then — surprise! — getting a different response in person. Hurt feelings, and sometimes lawsuits, result.

It goes further. Middle-class African Americans who speak mainstream English are sometimes seen as Uncle Toms by other blacks, who may view the very act of such speech as "giving in" to the coercion of white society. Among many poor black youths, the idea of any access to the mainstream has become a bitter joke, and speaking Standard English is grounds for immediate ridicule. Meanwhile, in the ears of suburbia, the very sound of black English, with its lowered pitch and rounded-off consonants and high-flung

vowels, becomes a trumpet of illiteracy and crimi-
nality — or, to the young, a siren song of danger and
rebellion.

Language, like artillery, carries a charge. And we
aim it, however unintentionally, at one another's
heads. When we make assumptions about one another on subways and in stores and in offices, much
more is at stake than mere speech.

The recent national firefight over "Ebonics" is a
perfect, though in some ways ridiculous, example.
The first shot went off when the Oakland, California,
school board voted in December 1996 to recognize
Ebonics (a name contrived by combining *ebony*
with *phonics*) as the primary language of African-
American students. Rocket explosions ensued. Prominent black intellectuals, including Harvard scholar
Henry Louis Gates, Jr., and poet and author Maya
Angelou, lined up to torpedo the idea. Others rushed
forward to defend it. Amid the uproar, the Oakland
board softened ("clarified" was the official word) its
position, and in the end the board's Ebonics gambit
looked for all the world much more like an imagina-
tive bid for badly needed funding than a philosophi-
cal stand for the black vernacular.

But in its vehemence, the debate laid bare the essential issue for many African Americans in this business of "good" and "bad" speech: defending the
beleaguered black psyche against the weapon of language. It is an old story, but one that has still not reg-
istered with most Americans. Just as throughout

history wars, such as England's Norman Conquest, have broken previous linguistic ties by imposing a conqueror's tongue, the forced dislocation of West Africans to the New World undermined black identity by attacking the languages that expressed it. Slaveowners learned early that controlling their "property" meant outlawing African languages (as well as African music and cultural traditions). Slaves were literally and figuratively battered with the message that African speech was not only backward but criminal, and that the language and culture of white Americans were superior. Slaves rebelled by using secret systems of speech, often as code, that preserved aspects of African languages, and combined them with vernacular, often regional, English. It was an act of creativity that continues to this day. So does the unmistakable message that white speech patterns and behavior are more desirable than black ones.

To a greater extent than white Americans, African Americans understand explicitly that speaking "white" English is a prerequisite to being taken seriously (outside of pop music and the NBA) by the American mainstream. Blacks also understand that speaking "black" English is more or less a guarantee of being stereotyped as poor, ignorant, and possibly dangerous. While analogous in some ways, the experiences of other immigrant groups are very different in that they lack the legacies of slavery and racial segregation. Irish Americans, for instance, were much maligned and oppressed in their early years here but never knew the systematic discrimination of Jim Crow, or the indelible brand of inferiority by skin color. Ultimately they were better able to merge with the mainstream, shedding their traditional speech along the way.

None of this, of course, is absolute: people of all backgrounds hold on to pieces of traditional vernacular. But having options makes all the difference. For many black Americans, for whom traditional paths of assimilation have been blocked — first by blanket discrimination and then by a lack of jobs and funding for public education — resentment at being ridiculed as an isolated subculture runs deep. And I mean *deep*. To many African Americans, being mocked for speaking black English feels like being called a savage all over again.

The result is what you might expect. In many poor black communities today, children who speak Standard English, or who embrace scholarship and the hope of upward mobility, are derided by other kids for "acting white." Within the college-educated African-American middle class, Standard English is embraced (with varying degrees of grammatical correctness) as the coin of the realm. At the same time, most black middle-class Americans, like me, hold on to black English as a way of being "down" among other black folk, using black expressions and inflections to cement the cultural bonds we share.

But, having become in effect bilingual, middle-class blacks take umbrage when a nonblack stranger assumes they speak only black English. This can be a handkerchief-headed denial of one's origins ("I ain't one of *them,* boss!") or it can be a justified rejection of an outrageous stereotype.

The amount of typecasting African Americans encounter defies belief. Once, for example, I hired a video production company in another city to do some work for one of my clients. As happens routinely in advertising production, I hired them sight unseen, choosing them on the strength of their previous work and on our numerous phone conversations. Finally, the time came for us to meet in person at their facility. I was accompanied on the trip by a white producer, whom I had also hired. The company representative, who was white, greeted us in the lobby by extending his hand enthusiastically to the white producer and calling him by my name. After weeks of phone conversations, he was utterly confident that this was the man who had hired him. And he was utterly embarrassed when he learned otherwise. Like so many others, he held racial preconceptions about authority. And without the cue of "black" speech on the telephone, he was lost.

Small daily assumptions are just as common. White salespeople and gas station attendants and doormen cock their heads to a black man with, "Help you, yo?" after having wished a white customer to "have a nice day, ma'am." White receptionists spell out directions to the eighth floor for a black woman with exaggerated slowness, as if translating English for the uninitiated. It is a routine ordeal of laughable absurdity. After all, would a white clerk who greets a black man with "Help you, yo?" also greet an Asian customer by mimicking a Chinese accent?

But there are other, deeper questions here. How should we treat black English when we hear it? Should we take the idea of Ebonics as a formal tongue seriously? Standard American English, after all, is not much closer to the King's English than Ebonics. I once heard a novelist observe, while talking about the peculiarities of American language, that the French version of his latest book carried the inscription "translated from the American" (as opposed to "the English"). All languages evolve continuously. And linguists agree that there is an unmistakably systematic structure to Ebonics. A commonly cited example (this from linguist John R. Rickford) is its five forms of the present tense: "He runnin'" ("He is running"), "He be runnin'" ("He is usually running"), "He be steady runnin'" ("He is usually running in an intensive, sustained manner"), "He bin runnin'" ("He has been running"), and "He BIN runnin'" ("He has been running for a long time and still is"). Given all of this, and the historical reasons why black English has been ghettoized, shouldn't we be willing to recognize it as an official language?

Not a chance. While linguists continue to debate the nature of Ebonics (most agree it is a dialect), the fact remains that it is a form of nonstandard English in a nation in which Standard English is the rule. And by the measure of Standard English, much of black English — like the English spoken by many uneducated whites — is poor English. There is no racial element in a white person saying to her white boss, "Where you gonna be at?" or "I ain't got none." She speaks that way because she has not learned to speak otherwise. To the extent that she is allowed to remain untutored in Standard English, her opportunities in life will be diminished, just as they are for millions of African Americans. We do children no favors by assigning official status to a vernacular when what they really need, beyond their everyday speech, is mastery of the language of the marketplace. Whether Ebonics can be a tool for moving students toward standard English is a question for educators. But for us to accept any goal short of competency in Standard English — being bilingual, if you like — flies in the face of common sense.

I was raised by college-educated parents, both of whom were reared in the North. Both speak Standard English with no recognizable "black" accent; not surprisingly, so do I. This is not an affect. I came by it naturally, as did my parents, both of whose families spoke in this manner. Speaking this way does not make me better or smarter or more sophisticated than a speaker of black English. It has, however, given me choices about how to make myself understood. It has extended my communicative reach. And isn't that why we have language?

Black or white, you can appreciate the history, depth, and beauty of black English while insisting on fluency in Standard English. We needn't treat it as a proposition of professor-talk versus felon-talk. If you're white, listen to black English as you would any dialect, and hear the keen colors and meanings it brings to the language, its creativity and precision. And hear that Standard English can rest gracefully right alongside on the same tongue. Here is celebrated African-American novelist Zora Neale Hurston, from her 1937 masterpiece *Their Eyes Were Watching God*:

[Pheoby said,] "Most of dese zigaboos is so het up over yo' business till they liable to hurry theyself to Judgment to find out about you if they don't soon know. You better make haste and tell 'em 'bout you and Tea Cake gittin' married, and if he taken all yo' money and went off wid some young gal, and where at he is now and where at is all yo' clothes dat you got to come back here in overhalls."

And here is Hurston again, on the next page:

They sat there in the fresh young darkness close together. Pheoby eager to feel and do through Janie, but hating to show her zest for fear it might be thought mere curiosity. Janie full of that oldest human longing — self-revelation.

Pheoby held her tongue for a long time, but she couldn't help moving her feet. So Janie spoke.

There was only one Zora Neale Hurston. There are as many more potential colors of speech as there are African Americans — or whites or Hispanics or Asians. Spend time with the verse of African-American poet Yusef Komunyakaa (his *Neon Vernacular* collection won the Pulitzer Prize), and his orchestra of voices will leave your ears ringing. Read the novels of Susan Straight (including *The Gettin' Place* and *Blacker Than a Thousand Midnights*), which vividly portray the interior of black life and language. She's white. Or check out African-American critic and columnist Greg Tate, author of the book *Flyboy in the Buttermilk*, who blends the black vernacular with other influences in an intellectually fierce style all his own. All of these writers have distinctive messages and singular voices. If you came to their work with any preconception of how a "black voice" is supposed to sound, you would miss the mark by miles. Every time.

The same applies to everyday language. If you are white, understand that use of black English says no more and no less about the speaker's character than your speech says about yours. If you are black, understand that the same applies to Standard English. Yes, some blacks are ashamed of their blackness and try to "act white" by denying their heritage in a variety of ways. But merely being fluent in a language —be it Standard English or Arabic — is no measure of a person. To make such a judgment, you have to look more deeply into their behavior and beliefs.

In any case, never presume to try to "speak someone's language" based on their appearance. In casual encounters, speak in your normal manner unless you have a compelling reason to do otherwise — say, while traveling in Spain. Avoid making assumptions about ethnicity from phone conversations, unless a specific accent is so unmistakable as to put the matter beyond doubt. Even then you could be wrong. And the conversational hole you will have to dig yourself out of may be deep. As a black American who is often greeted with such foolish attempts at "translation," I find the best response is to simply reply in my ordinary way of speaking. This straightens people up quickly.

Whatever your race, you have no right to pipe up and correct the grammar of an adult unless you have reason to believe that your input will be constructive and welcomed. As for correcting a child's speech, it must be done, if at all, by the child's own parent, guardian, or teacher. It is not your place to step in and play grammarian unless you know that the parent would wish you to do so.

My own favorite summary of the black English controversy comes from Henry Louis Gates, Jr., who joked about how his own father declared that the entire Ebonics quarrel was "modiculous" and that he was "regusted" with the whole thing. Sadly, however, the fiery debate over black English ultimately misses the point. Ebonics or no Ebonics, what black schools need is the money and the resources to teach a generation of increasingly alienated African-American children. The real questions, in Oakland and nationwide, are these: Why are inner-city schools being allowed to crumble? Why are employment markets in black communities perpetually at depression levels, sapping students of any hope for jobs and careers? And, as I recently heard one African-American scholar ask, why are so many black children closing ranks, in their language and their values, within a cynical subculture that is increasingly isolated from, and hostile toward, the mainstream?

Let's add *that* to our black and white talk.

11

"Black" Jokes, Polish Jokes, and George Jefferson: Who Are We Laughing At?

> A black man walks into a bar with a parrot on his shoulder. The bartender says, "Hey, where'd you get that?" The parrot says, "Africa."
>
> — A joke making the rounds

> "... And that's why darkies were born."
>
> — Groucho Marx, at the end of a frenzied monologue in *Duck Soup*

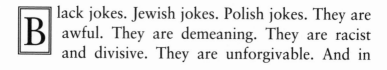 lack jokes. Jewish jokes. Polish jokes. They are awful. They are demeaning. They are racist and divisive. They are unforgivable. And in

just the right context and the right company, some of them are funny. Every black person, every Jew, every Pole — except for those who have boiled away their capacity for irony — knows this. And that's the problem. Because while we may be more than willing to laugh at ourselves in the warmth of safe company, we are *not* willing to fling wide the doors and invite others to laugh at us. We know that what might be a wicked little joke in our own self-protective hands is, in the hands of someone who does not mean well, a weapon.

You could call this two-sided attitude toward jokes hypocrisy. I call it survival. When popular culture or the media and entertainment industries indulge in racial or ethnic stereotype, the injured parties naturally resist by trying to take charge of their own image. At the same time, they reserve the right to poke their own innards, or even (if they so choose) to diss themselves unmercifully.

Q: How do you stop black kids from jumping up and down on the bed?
A: Put Velcro on the ceiling.

When one of my sisters, whose black self-esteem and love of children are unshakable, once leaned over conspiratorially and told me that joke, we both laughed and winced. We laughed not because we like to demean black children but because we are incapable of doing so — because we were once black

127

children ourselves, grimacing when our mother pulled a plastic comb through our oiled hair; because, to our eyes, nothing can *stop* a nappy-headed black kid from being beautiful. Least of all the outrageous image of being stuck momentarily to the ceiling.

But when a white man with a fake mustache and an unlit cigar turns to the camera, as Groucho Marx does in *Duck Soup,* to deliver a throwaway line about "darkies," I do not laugh. Nor have I ever, in all of the times I have seen that classic film, heard anyone else laugh at that line. A quick put-down from a smart-assed white man, who knows or cares little about actual black people, is not funny; it's just a plain old racist put-down.

To be fair to Groucho, some context is in order. He came straight out of vaudeville, which also produced Al Jolson, and he worked in an era in which the stereotype was king. In the 1930s, making "darkie" jokes and staging chorus scenes of dancing black cotton pickers (as in the Marx Brothers film *A Day at the Races*) was considered solid entertainment for white audiences. I doubt, however, that blacks laughed at those scenes then. And I hear no whites laughing now.

When it comes to ethnic jokes, thoughtful people should entertain a kind of unofficial etiquette. They may not always follow it, but they basically believe in it. Call it the Masturbation Rule: when it comes to indulging in ethnic humor, the privilege of self-abuse belongs, ultimately, to the affected group alone. All others, while they may dare to chortle over the foibles of the Polish or Jewish or black guy who walks into a bar, do so at their own bloody peril. It is a good rule.

A predominantly Jewish or black audience howls at a Jewish or black stand-up comic's ethnic inside joke because it *understands*. Mixed with the humor, however cruel, is knowledgeable empathy and un-threatened self-esteem. If as an outsider you lack this understanding, your laughter becomes literally op-pressive. Show me a white person telling a black joke with no black person in sight, and I'll show you a per-son who likely has few or no black friends, who has almost no personal knowledge of black people, who is probably not comfortable being around black people, and who, worse, somehow thinks that his or her own racial ignorance and discomfort are perfectly acceptable.

That's what is wrong, in fact, with most of the so-called black TV characters and sitcoms that amuse so many of us. The sassing, gassing, sashaying, mutu-ally dissing black characters of prime-time television, from *Amos 'n' Andy* to *The Jeffersons* to *Booty Call*, are, in effect, a black joke told by a white-dominated media — with the help of career-savvy black stars and writers and producers willing to cash in on a trend. Viewers, game for familiar formulas and easy laughs, get the same mouth-flapping black brothers and sarcastic black sisters and troubled black cops in show after show, all justified by marketing surveys showing that of all the (single) options available, black viewers pick *this* one. And for a wholesome alternative, there are always sitcom varieties of Cosby Knows Best. With few exceptions, that's the selection. It's not that we should replace these formulaic minstrel shows with antiseptic politically approved skits. And it's not that the jokes on these shows are never funny. It's that there is not a black voice — the voice of a broader variety of black experience — doing the telling. And, for me, it is hard to laugh at "nigger" jokes told by white television executives — even with black actors as mouthpieces.

But wait. I hear a white person objecting, "Why all of the carrying on about black humor? You've admitted that everyone is a fair target for ethnic jokes: Jews, Italians, Poles, Scandinavians. This is America. We're *all* capable of being turned into cartoon characters. What's the big deal?"

Well, see, the thing is, we are *not* all cartoon characters. I challenge you to tell me *one* "white" joke. I don't mean a joke about a specific ethnic or cultural or physical subgroup of whites — WASPs, Poles, Germans, hillbillies, blonds. I mean a joke that makes fun of the broad, generally understood American idea of being white, in the same way that a black joke makes fun of the very idea of being black. Have you heard many such white jokes recently? I'll bet you haven't. Because, as we have all had drummed into us, most recently by television, whiteness is not in and of itself remarkable or funky or quaint. Whiteness is therefore not funny. It is featureless. It is invisible. It is the norm.

Tell a Polish joke, any Polish joke, even the most vulgar one imaginable. When you have finished, and the laughter has faded, the Polish farmer in the punch line strolls out of the joke and back onto the street, where he melds into the blanket identity of whiteness. In the sidewalk crowd he is no longer seen as the butt of a Polish joke. He is a white guy. But what about the guy in the black joke? What about the black guy with the parrot on his shoulder? When he escapes the punch line and strolls onto the street, he is still seen as the character in the joke: a guy dumb enough to be led around by a bird. He cannot merge with the throng of normalcy. He remains separate, noticed, "a black guy." And everybody knows what *that* means.

This is the setting within which you or I or anyone else tells a black joke. No wonder, then, that to some African Americans any humor at their expense is unacceptable, and any such humor expressed by a black person is treason. And no wonder that so many of us have strict rules of engagement about such jokes, even when they happen to make us laugh. We know the damage that they can do in unfriendly hands. And *that's* not funny.

Hence the Masturbation Rule: abuse yourself up to the limits of what you are able to tolerate and defend. Abuse others at your own profound risk. Which means, if you're black, you can tell a black joke and, at the very worst, expect to fight or talk your way out of it. And if you're white, you cannot.

It's a good rule because it rests on ownership. The state of being black belongs to black people, and if you are an African American, your particular state of being black belongs to you. No one, black or white, can define the terms of your racial self-respect. No one can decree that you can't laugh at such-and-such and still like yourself, or that you can't say so-and-so and still love being black. It's your call to make. If you decide that your identity can handle the tension of chuckling at a sinfully awful black joke, laugh. And be prepared for any accusations of blasphemy.

If you are white, blackness is not yours to abuse in the first place. Unless you are so comfortable with African-American friends that you know you can take liberties among them, keep your hands off black jokes. Maybe you simply cannot resist the naughty little pleasure; if so, the mere transgression doesn't necessarily make you a racist. But do you have any black friends? Do you hang around with African Americans enough to know anything firsthand about black life? Or is your image of black people a collection of sitcom fragments, NBA games, and observations from across subway platforms? If you snicker at a punch line while remaining ignorant about African Americans, you have made a joke of racial understanding itself. And that's a worse crime than all the black jokes in the world.

Head to Head,
Heart to Heart

12

A State of Being Sorry

o you know me?

I am a certain black male who always some-how seems to be apologetic. You may have noticed.

For much of my life, in fact, I have apologized too much. Much too much. This has been pointed out to me by friends and by those not so friendly, both gently and stridently. After denying it for as long as was comfortably possible, I decided to investigate both my own behavior and that of my cultural broth-ers. In the hallways and on the streets, in elevators and in arenas, I began to pay attention. And damned if my critics didn't turn out to be right.

Whether you have noticed or not, there is a

certain approval-hungry quality to being black, male, and repentant — most keenly evident among the genial, educated black males whom the rest of the world regards as astonishingly nice guys. It is a manner that has nothing at all to do with good manners.

Let me tell you what I mean.

I watch us, you see — sometimes dressed in jeans, but usually in suits and ties — I see us, in this long, white entry corridor, apologizing our way through life, "bobbing and weaving our way down the street," as I once heard a black psychologist say, accidentally bumping into someone, especially a white someone, and blurting out the most hurried, heartfelt, and excessive stream of apologies for barely having brushed an arm or a purse; crossing paths with an oncoming someone, especially a white someone, and immediately and unconsciously yielding while uttering repentant regrets; expertly maneuvering, staying clear, dancing through, avoiding and denying the glances of fear and resentment that slashingly remind us of the depth to which we are mistrusted.

This is no accident, this apoplexy of apologizing, no product of good home training. Like most of our dearly held ideas of how to behave, it has to do with our very stance as black men in this particular place at this particular time.

I watch us graciously and conspicuously thanking an oblivious waiter for the silverware, then the napkin, then the water, the bread, the iced tea, the entrée, the dessert, and finally even the check; hurrying to excuse ourselves when one of us politely coughs or sneezes or clears our throat or even inaudibly sniffs. Apologizing, apologizing — for having been in the way of someone who was also in our way, for unintentionally unsettling or startling someone, for having misunderstood a trivial thing that could have been better explained, for having asked the store clerk for the wrong brand of soap when the sign was misleading, for any of a thousand flyspeck foibles.

I watch us, day after day, apologizing all up and down our college-educated behinds as we dolefully make our way through the obstacle courses of our lives. I see us apologizing, when all is said and done, for simply being black and male and misunderstood. I see us apologizing for who we are wrongly perceived to be, and struggling through our unintentionally exaggerated public displays of politeness, to let these misguided white people know, once and for all, that we are *nice guys,* that we are *all right,* even by the rigorously bland standards of American culture.

After all, we educated black men have good table manners and sound personal principles and Lysol in the bathroom and clean underwear beneath our slacks. We are not, despite the clutching of purses and keys and hip pockets that ripples through a crowd as we pass, going to rob or beat or rape Caucasian descendants of slaveowners and indentured servants and immigrants. Whether they believe it or not, we are following paths of our own, paths that will allow them to retain possession of their lives and their property and even their privacy. And the more the clutching at purses and stereotypes persists, the more loudly we acceptance-starved, respectable black males feel the need to apologize for our state of mistaken identity:

Please, look at me. Listen to me. Watch me hold the door for you. Pay attention as I generously tip the waiter. Notice as I come within inches of your purse without showing any inclination whatsoever to rob or accost you. Hear me speak proper English — educated English, English that speaks of intellectual achievement and seriousness of purpose — as I address you. See me walk past you in a fine suit and climb into a car that only a professional could afford. You still do not see? You do not understand? You cannot make out who I am? Oh, excuse me. I am sorry. I beg your pardon. I'll try again.

It is like taking the childhood lessons of my upbringing and amplifying them to soul-splitting volume: there is no virtue greater than being "nice," no sin more venal than being "not nice." To entertain a nasty or cruel notion about someone, or to take a pigheaded position on a subject, becomes not merely wrong or unfair but, worse, "not nice." Niceness is the way in, niceness is the admission card to the mainstream, the antidote to one's own toxicity as a black male in a society that presumes all black males to be poisonous. *Yes, you should be intelligent, you should be ambitious, you should be honorable. But you absolutely* must *be nice.*

And so we spread out across the countryside, we hordes of smart and successful black American men, working so very hard at being nice. By the time we reach adulthood, we are nice by instinct, nice by reflex, nice without even meaning to be nice. We are so nice that we forget how to fight, so nice that we forget that the territory within our skins belongs to us, so nice that even a whiff of disapproval from the wider world can send us backpedaling in a catechismic flurry of apology. It is almost as if, with our singular black selves, we take on all of the world's sorriness for racism, sorriness for rage, sorriness for misunderstanding. If we are sorry enough — we seem to say — maybe it will all go away.

We can take a lesson — a thoughtful lesson, one that does not treat suicide and survival as fashion statements, as do some of my middle-class black friends with their BMWs and backward baseball caps — from the yo boys, the bangers, whose single most liberating reality amid a life of fostered self-endangerment is the ability to simply say "Fuck you" to the very culture that so strangles the black middle class. We can take a lesson from our tortured but honest little brothers, who meet the clutching of purses and pockets with smoldering stares that say, I can use your fear against you. We can apologize less, save our thanks for deserving waiters, stand our ground more. We can begin to live less for others' understanding of us, and more for our own.

We might find that it feels nice.

So much of this apologizing by black gentlemen, after all, does have to do with lost rage: *No, I am not going to brutalize you, although maybe I should.* It is not that men such as us are strangers to anger. It is that we know anger all too well, and we are not willing to let it dominate our public persona. The more bestial the received stereotype of black men, the stiffer our resolve to override it through mild-mannered respectability. It is a hopelessly lost cause for everyone, black and white, because the rage belongs to us all, and it is not going to go away.

The rage is like a heavy metal — mercury or uranium — that long ago leached into the viscera of black and white Americans on Virginia slave docks and has been part of us ever since, sickening, elusive. I watch us constantly hand it off to one another, like handfuls of roiling poison. A white man buys black slaves and lies to himself about their humanity. Three hundred years later, a black teenager glares at a white driver in traffic. Across town, one white woman tells another that black men are scary. In an office tower a few miles away, a black executive carries himself with exaggerated gentility and propriety.

And what if the very fear displayed by whites toward blacks reveals whites' unwitting acceptance of the basis for black rage? Sometimes, when I observe whites grabbing their personal belongings in the presence of African Americans, the entire scene seems like a metaphor for a guilty white conscience: the former slaveholder who once trafficked in stolen human property now anxiously guarding his possessions from the scrutiny of the freed slave. I wonder if such small acts of defensiveness sometimes betray a subconscious white voice: *If I were black and living in the aftermath of having been enslaved, I'd be mad. I might want to take something back as revenge. Hey, where is my wallet, anyway?*

Apologies, apologies: from black American men, from white American presidents. Bill Clinton is sorry for slavery; a black man on an elevator is sorry for being mistaken for a caged predator. Have the mea culpas and the grins done us any good? Are any of us, as a result, any less angry? Any less threatened? Any better paid? Any better understood? Just as our response to the national crisis of race must be national political action, not a show of collective sorrow, our solution to our daily mini-crises of race must be personal action.

Understand me. I am not positing individual action as a convenient personal substitute for politics; I am positing it as a part of politics. The politics of racial conflict do not stop at your doorway. They begin there. We must be pissed-off and curious and fearless not from a distance but where it counts: up close, in elevators, in long lines at supermarkets, in the kitchens of in-laws, in conversation and argument, in car-repair shops, in subway cars. It is precisely in these countless throwaway encounters — the ones in which we presume real racial contact to be unthinkable — that such contact becomes, in fact, vital.

Imagine: in an elevator, the formerly apologetic black man peers at a nervous white stranger and asks, in a deep and even tone of voice, "What are *you* so afraid of?" Or, as did a black male friend of mine in the face of a purse-clutching white woman, he turns the tables by clasping his own briefcase to his chest in a parody of her fear. A white man catches a flash of seemingly racial ire from a black coworker, and rather than backpedaling away from yet another "black thing," asks him what his problem is. A black woman does the same thing with a white acquaintance. A white woman, caught in the heat of a black youth's defiant glance on the subway, pauses to think beyond her own grip on her bag to imagine what sort of security this bristling child has lost — or never known.

It is not rage that we should be worrying about. A mere century and a half after slavery, with the race issue serving as a national punching bag, we *ought* to feel hounded by rage. Among blacks, only the walking dead could be free of anger over race, and among scared whites who see no reason to empathize, resentment is inescapable. How could it be otherwise? Did we really think that blacks and whites could brush one another's skins and feel one another's breath in elevators and on sidewalks, free of pain, while hemorrhaging? If you are a black person, forced in a thousand daily ways to fend off — or succumb to — the continually flying shrapnel of slavery's aftermath, of course you are angry. If you are a white person, sucked into a conflict that began with a crime you personally had nothing to do with, of course you are angry.

The danger is not in our having rage, but in our failing to confront one another in close personal quarters, with weapons safely out of reach. The danger is in our feeling, instead, obligated to be secretive, or to be sorry, or to be "nice." As if our racial relationships can bear nothing more. But maybe the truth is that our racial relationships cannot bear so little. And maybe we had better ask more of ourselves in our daily crossing of paths.

If we do not, we might be sorry.

13

The Black Ambassador

I *t is a title conferred every day upon individual African Americans without their permission: "Ambassador for Black People Everywhere." It bestows the responsibility upon black people, any time and anywhere, to enlighten well-intentioned nonblacks about the black point of view — as in, "Why do so many black people feel that —?" or, "What is black people's opinion of —?" The topic could be anything, although it usually reflects the standard palette of black-related issues offered up by mainstream media coverage: crime, affirmative action, crime, celebrities, crime, sports, crime. From the questioner's standpoint, this is all perfectly innocent;*

when you have few or no black friends and little un-
derstanding of black life, you open whatever win-
dows you can. And who better to ask for help than an
African American?

But that's the problem. You are asking *an* African American: one person, with one set of experiences, one heart, and one brain. Here he or she is, minding his or her own business on the bus or at work, and suddenly he or she is asked to step in for millions of black folk. The temptation is to snap, "Why are you asking *me?*"

Look, it's not wrong for a well-meaning white person to seek out a black person's opinion. It's wrong, though, to treat that opinion as anything other than one person's view. The unspoken assumption behind a what-do-black-people-think interrogation ("One black opinion is the same as any other, so I'll ask you") is aggravating beyond belief. Imagine the gall of, say, a foreigner asking a white American "how white people feel" about antipoverty programs. *Which* white people? Those staffing food kitchens for homeless families? Those playing golf with owners of sweatshops? Those wearing swastikas? As I once heard Henry Louis Gates, Jr., say in a radio interview, "There are 32 million African Americans. That means there are 32 million ways of *being* an African American." So, too, for the 216 million Americans who happen to be white.

Forget entirely about gaining any kind of broad knowledge about black folk from talking with one or two people. There are no shortcuts. If you want to know what one black friend thinks about something, ask him or her. If you want to know what a lot of black people think, ask a lot of black people. And if you really want to know how deep and how wide the river of discourse runs, check out the world of African-American books, magazines, journals, newspapers, on-line resources, and television and radio programs. From the magazine *Ebony,* for instance, you might conclude that all African Americans worship celebrity and aspire to become middle managers for large corporations. From the Nation of Islam's newspaper, *The Final Call,* you might think that all black people study African languages, eschew pork, and embrace political separatism. From Shelby Steele's book *The Content of Our Character,* you might infer that all black Americans live in the suburbs and oppose affirmative action. None of these generalizations, of course, is true. How could *any* such sweeping statement be true?

I have black friends who, to this day, when cornered to defend some blanket statement that they have made about white people, will say, "Oh, come on. You know how *they* are." But I do not know how "they" are. Neither do you, nor do any of us. It is our hip-pocket miracle as black and white Americans that we are generally able, in spite of daily pressure to rush out of our homes and butcher one another, instead to blunder onward toward possible collective survival. On that score, the race card is a useless guide to virtue.

Several years ago, I gave a poetry reading at which the white hostess introduced me to the mostly white crowd as a poet who would bring into the room "the black man's angry rhythms of the street" or some such patronizing nonsense. I had no idea who she was talking about. I proceeded, through my poems, to present a clearer vision of my landscape, which includes wind-scoured Alaskan tundra as well as steaming pavement, and in which I have furiously slaughtered fish with my father as well as smiled gratefully at a passing church lady. My hostess let on to no disappointment, but I am certain that she, having clearly only taken a cursory look at my work, had been expecting some spokesman for Authentic Black Urban Angst rather than an actual human being. I was, after all, black, male, and sneakered. What else was there for her to know?

The epitome of this kind of blunder is the way in which many whites view black celebrities. By the "black ambassador" treatment, Colin Powell, a general with views significantly to the right of most black Americans, becomes a "black figure" whose opinions are deemed important for race relations. Oprah Winfrey, a woman of dazzling opinion and even more dazzling wealth, becomes a reference point for "what blacks are saying." Michael Jordan, the galaxy's greatest basketball player, becomes an icon of black poise and athleticism.

To be sure, much of the power of such mega-celebrity has little to do with the "credit-to-their-race" syndrome. Oprah, for instance, did not take on the cattle industry as a black woman; she took them on as an antidisease advocate, period. Her fans, of all colors, love her not because she is black, but because she is Oprah. The same universal glamour applies to Powell, Jordan, and many other black celebrities.

Still, some whites have a tendency (perhaps without even knowing it) to try to entrap Oprah, or Colin, or the black woman across the hall into speaking for all black Americans at moments of racial doubt. And despite blacks' proportionately greater exposure to a variety of white opinions, some blacks persist in treating whites the same way. In either case, it is a losing proposition: little knowledge gained, much ignorance preserved.

Whatever my color, whatever my history or my communal memory, it comes down to this: Want to know what I think? Ask me and I'll tell you. Want to know what all "people like me" think? Forget it. End of conversation.

14

Are You Calling Me a *Racist?*

A *true story: During my childhood in the 1960s,* *our household presented, to many in the sur-* *rounding community of middle-class whites,* *hard actual evidence that black folk did not reside in* *trees. Once, my mother and a white neighbor were in* *the middle of a mildly political conversation when the* *white woman suddenly put down her coffee cup,* *peered earnestly at my mother, and asked, "Why am I* *afraid of black people?" My mother looked serenely* *back at her. "Because you're a racist," she answered.*

Another true story: A friend of mine, who is *white, has a sister-in-law who is black. One day my* *friend, who as it happens has a long history of send-* *ing cute animal greeting cards to her brother, picked out a typically precious card featuring a photograph of an orangutan. Since she knew the couple was expecting a child, she inscribed the card with a whimsical message to her brother about his impending fatherhood. She mailed the card. Days later, her black sister-in-law telephoned, furious: "How dare you send a card with a monkey on it!"*

Memories of high school science notwithstanding (orangutans are apes, not monkeys), I was of no help to my friend after she finished telling me her story. She was pained; I was laughing. Her questions for me were: (1) Had she been insensitive? and (2) How in the world was she ever going to pick out another card for this woman? My only question, which I tried to put tactfully, was whether the sister-in-law was in therapy and, if not, why not.

Two very different stories, from two different eras. In the first, a white person dares to bare feelings she is ashamed of, and a black person dares to reply truthfully, at the risk of poisoning a friendly relationship. In the second story, a black person lashes out, offended, and the shocked white person struggles to react, torn between self-doubt and common sense. Certainly, thirty years ago an orangutan card would have been the least of a typical interracial couple's social problems. But in other respects, either episode could have happened today.

Both raise the same question: How do we lay it on the line to each other, as blacks and whites, without exposing ourselves to merciless shame or, worse, creating a war? How do you know when to tell your white neighbor that she is a racist, or to tell your black sister-in-law that she is paranoid?

The answer is that if we all waited until we knew we were right before opening our mouths, allowing ourselves zero risk of misunderstanding or overstatement, then nothing worthwhile would ever get said. It's just not that easy. Change requires risk. There are leaps to be made, conversational licks to be taken. What has so many well-intentioned white and black people either stammering or seething is the half-witted notion that we cannot afford to be racially in error, cannot afford to be corrected, cannot abide conflict or argument and still sustain a racial dialogue.

So once conversation has been sufficiently stifled — as it has today, both by resentful eye-rolling and outright public bluster — there is really only one way through: engagement. You have to risk being taken for a judgmental white racist or an apologist for black dysfunction. Maybe that's what you actually are. Maybe you deserve to have it flung back in your face. Perhaps you need a good rocking and rolling, a healthy little bang of criticism. Or maybe, on the other hand, the other party should not be spared what you hold clenched in your fist. Perhaps somebody needs to be called out. And perhaps, when all is said and done, everyone survives.

My mother's white friend could have taken the easy way out. She did not have to admit to a black person that she was afraid of black people. And she certainly did not have to be willing to explore *why* she feared black people. She could have done what a million white people would have done: smiled, finished her coffee without comment, and counted the money in her purse the minute my mother left. Instead, she took a personal risk and spoke up. So did my mother, who, rather than smoothing over a horribly awkward moment with a conciliatory reply, plunged straight into the ugly heart of the matter. The resulting conversation taught them both something about unexpected potential. Over the ensuing years, they never became close friends. But they probably never would have anyway. The point is that their brutal honesty on that day did not end their relationship. It may have even helped them to sustain it.

Not that happy endings are assured. As I said, this is all about risk. I cannot imagine the orangutan affair ending with anything like harmony, let alone hugs. And yet, it had to happen the way it did. The white woman, having a perfectly happy history of sending animal cards to her brother, never even thought about race. The black sister-in-law's incensed reply caught the white woman at her most vulnerable point: her awareness that she does not know what it feels like to be black. She was trapped. Her instincts told her that her sister-in-law was being ridiculous. But her fear of being shamed as a racist prevented her from trusting herself: "What if I'm wrong? What if she had a right to be offended? How can I know for certain?"

In fact, she could not know for sure. When she got the angry phone call, she had to make a decision based on uncertainty. She could trust herself and take the heat: "Orangutan? Nigger joke? Excuse me? Woman, what *are* you talking about?" Or she could disobey her instincts and fold: "I didn't mean it that way. I apologize." Either way, she risked making a mistake. There was no protection, no guarantee.

But that is precisely the reason to engage. The reality is inescapable: most of the time, you simply cannot know in advance whether you will end up being right or wrong. You cannot know whether you will improve the prospects for friendship or make an enemy. There are too many surprises hidden within racial dialogue. And so the only thing to do is try, and to accept the risks — of hard feelings, of racial blunders — as the cost of a process that in the long run draws us closer together.

One night at a Thai restaurant in Amsterdam, a waiter was about to seat me when the maître d' hastily interfered. He pointed ruefully to his watch: it was ten o'clock, he said. Closing time. He was sorry but very firm. He could seat no more customers. I was hungry. I was alone. I looked around at the room packed with European faces, and I snapped back bitterly, automatically, "Would it be closed if I were *white?*" The maître d' stared dumbly at me for a moment, and then he suddenly saw how the pieces fit and smiled, saying gently, "No, oh no, I am not like that. It's not what you think." His sincerity was unassailable. He asked me if I would please come back tomorrow; he promised I would not be disappointed. I felt a sickening sense of embarrassment at myself. I apologized for my hastiness, and I returned the next night — before ten o'clock — and was rewarded with a fine meal and warm treatment. It's not that there is no racism in Amsterdam; there is plenty of it. I had simply picked the wrong establishment in which to take offense. Had I not made my ill-fated show of indignation, I would never have learned that I was wrong about that restaurant and, no doubt, wrong about a good deal more. I carried the lesson back home.

On another occasion, while working as a copywriter at an advertising agency, I noticed that a particular white art director with whom I was paired never seemed to include people of color in his ads. The two of us would come up with an idea for a campaign — with no mention of race — and when he came back with layouts and TV storyboards, all of the characters would be white. All of the time. Finally, I said something about it. He listened. He politely bristled. He said race wasn't the kind of thing he thought about. He said he didn't see it as an issue. I replied that it *was* an issue; not everyone in our target audience was white. He didn't say much in response. Our conversation pretty much ended there. But soon

thereafter, people of color began to appear in his layouts.

Get in the game already. Realize that your only
hope for any kind of peace with this business of
racism is to understand that confrontation need not
lead to annihilation. You can survive offending a
sister-in-law or a coworker — at least when both con-
versants lack firearms. You can also survive being
wrong, and even learn from it. People will let you
know soon enough what they think of what you
think. But how do you expect to find out with your
mouth closed? Not that you should feel entitled to
fling around "Re-Legalize Slavery" or "Castrate White
People" proclamations with the expectation of pro-
moting reasoned dialogue. But at a certain point, like
it or not, you will have to trust your own idea of what
is reasonable, and go with it.

Do you think that a particular black-made film
was shallow and mean-spirited? Say so. Does it seem
to you that a certain white torch singer has ascended
to the stature of pop deity basically by lip-synching
the heartbreak-thin keening of Motown divas past?
Out with it. Has a prominent African-American ac-
tivist made statements that seem laughable to you?
Let's hear it. Is television's latest sassy-darkie or
sensitive-detective minstrel sitcom more than you can
bear? Don't hold back. From what I have seen of
racial card-folding among folks who ought to be ar-
guing, the most dangerous racist assumption is that
a black or white acquaintance "won't be able to

handle" disagreement or challenge. Please. While zealots are out bombing buildings and burning churches, the rest of us are afraid to talk because we might *upset* one another?

I say, let's talk while we still can.

15

Race to Nowhere:
The Ten Worst Racial Ideas of Black,
and White, Americans

With our American genius for generalization, you would think that blacks and whites would pause sometimes to look at some of the patently false things we have come to believe about one another. In that spirit, consider these ten-worst lists — one white, one black — compiled purely on the authority of personal observation, with absolutely no application whatsoever of the scientific method. Objectivity is not guaranteed.

The Ten Worst Ideas Held
by White People about Black People

1. Black people *want* to feel victimized.

Here is the line of reasoning: "African Americans are hooked on racial resentment. They have made it a religion. They blame everything on race, and use it as an excuse for not taking responsibility for themselves. No matter what they are given, they are never satisfied."

What a great way for a white person to avoid the real issues of racism: discrimination, double standards in criminal prosecution, poverty, health, education, police brutality, hate and violence, high blood pressure. Look, no black person *wants* to live with these threats. No black person *wants* to walk the earth with a significantly higher risk for heart attack and stroke. No black person *wants* to feel hopeless or resentful. Who would? Even to the extent that some blacks do plunge into obsessive race hate (however justified or unjustified their reasons), they constitute — like white supremacists — a minority whose desperation does not really qualify as a "choice" anyway.

Trying to deny the experience of the majority of black Americans will get you nowhere. Much racial deadlock, in fact, results from the simple refusal of whites to believe anything of what blacks are trying to tell them. To a fair-minded person, the real question is, Why are reasonable people up in arms about race, and what should we be doing about it?

2. When it comes to black people, there are "good" ones and "bad" ones.

This has always been one foul-smelling proposition, usually entertained by whites struggling to explain why they are not racists. On the surface, the mere act of distinguishing between "goodness" and "badness" may seem reasonable enough. But since when do any of us — aside from while making racial or other indefensible judgments — sum up any person as entirely good or bad? I have heard plenty of whites hem and haw about the good and the bad in the black population. But do they commonly talk about good and bad whites? Or Germans? Or Poles?

Come to think of it, why does a white person even need to remark upon "good" and "bad" blacks in the first place? It sounds as if what they really mean is, "I have to approach black people carefully, because a whole lot of them are bad." Suddenly, it's not so defensible a point of view, is it?

3. Blacks act as if slavery happened yesterday. They can't let go of it.

For a black person caught speeding ninety miles an hour to claim that slavery got him a traffic ticket is one thing. But let's look at the record. Slavery was outlawed in this country less than 150 years ago. Roughly two human beings, or ten dogs, or one tortoise, could live and die in that length of time. The period since legal slavery is just three times that since the end of World War II. It is barely twice the age of the American automobile. It is no time at all.

Let go of slavery? How could anyone think that we have escaped the impact of slavery? Or, to put it another way, when America lets go of the legacy of slavery — that is, when race has no bearing on access to a decent education, career prosperity, or the likelihood of ending up on death row — then black people too will forget about slavery. Until then, as racial tension and hate crimes continue, we can all expect to be reminded of slavery more or less daily.

4. Black people should be more appreciative of the racial progress we have all made.

We have, you could say, come a long way. Slavery is illegal. So are segregation and lynchings, although both are far from extinct. Our society is without question much more just now, and in important ways, than even fifty years ago.

But can a prisoner released to home detention feel that he is free? In many respects, ours is still two countries — in employment, in the incidence of poverty, in infant mortality, in law enforcement, in mood.

When the right to life, liberty, and the pursuit of a mortgage continues to be denied for racial reasons, a black stomach can feel half empty instead of half full. Unless, as for some, there is no food at all.

Look at it this way: rules are one thing; reality is another. If you are white, imagine how hard it would be for you to feel grateful for having been released from outright bondage into a life of mere unfairness. Perhaps you should work harder to meet African Americans halfway — by showing more appreciation of what they have endured.

5. You can't talk with an African American about race. They're too touchy.

Okay, so black Americans can be touchy sometimes. So can you. Disagree anyway. I mean, who came up with the fainthearted idea that blacks and whites will break out in hives when they disagree? I want to find our smilingly unbiased "harmony" consultants and slap them until they confess to having opinions. Slinking off silently does no one any good. Silence ensures that nothing changes. Honest dialogue means that someone learns. Maybe you, maybe someone else. Maybe both.

Make no mistake: conversation can hurt. But it certainly beats racial warfare. And if we stop talking, that's where we're heading.

6. When a black person succeeds, it is because he or she had help.

You know the attitude: that black female manager would never have nailed that position if the company hadn't been looking to promote an African-American woman. That black contractor is a national sensation, but he never would have gotten anywhere without minority set-asides. That black scholarship student seems bright and ambitious enough, but you know what *really* got him into Yale.

Let's not debate affirmative action again. The real problem here is that quotas or no quotas, job anxiety among whites in today's head-chopping corporate climate leads some to attack the abilities of practically all high-achieving blacks. I would suggest to such angry whites only that they look at the facts: how small the "problem" of "unqualified" minorities was, even in the heyday of affirmative action, before job security became an issue for whites. When job insecurity subsides, so will the fervor to blame job market problems on black bumblers.

7. When a black person fails, it is his or her own fault.

This enables some whites to have it both ways. They can say that middle-class blacks lack the qualifications for success, while also claiming that poor blacks deserve no help because they already have everything it takes to succeed. The villain becomes "government spending," and the poster child for the lack of "black responsibility" becomes the young unwed mother on welfare. None of this makes any sense. Most single mothers on welfare are white. They became pregnant with the help of men. Welfare is not their reason for poverty (lack of living-wage jobs and education is). And welfare accounts for only 2 percent of the federal budget (as opposed to the Pentagon's 16 percent share). Does that sound to you as if hordes of black welfare chiselers are breaking the back of the federal treasury? Again, when you look at the facts, the image of low-income black people as fat connivers disappears. Like smoke.

8. African Americans have one culture: "black."

This myth is what enables so many white Americans to search in vain for the "black point of view" or "what black people want." What is African-American culture? What is the experience of being black? Ask a black jazz musician who spends most of his time traveling and performing in Europe, Africa, and Asia. Then ask a black corporate manager who just bought a suburban home and who devours John Grisham novels. Then ask a black high school dropout who dreams of being a rap star. Then ask a street-corner dealer who nets eight thousand a week and has heart palpitations. Then ask Vernon Jordan. Then ask Michael Jackson.

It is the very breadth of black American culture that makes African Americans impossible to pigeon-hole. There is no one black social life any more than there is a white social life. There is no single "black" room to which all African Americans flock after work, where everyone talks the same talk and dreams the same dreams and listens to the same music. It just isn't so. If you are white, don't fool yourself into thinking that you know black people as a group. Instead, you know some people who are black.

9. Blacks are born dancers, athletes, and lovers.

Let's mention the unmentionable: there are more Magic Johnsons than Larry Birds. Any way you look at it, there is no white James Brown (with all due respect to my man Van Morrison), and there was no white John Coltrane or Billie Holiday. Black music, with its barrier-melting fusions of rhythmic and harmonic invention, has parental rights to much of the music that we call American. And it is clear, on any dance floor in the country, who has gotten a head start in the realm of spontaneously coordinated movement that we call popular dance.

But does any of this make African Americans into Jimmy the Greek's natural athletes or Hollywood's born tapmasters? Does it make blacks into bulging human vessels of joyful intuition and savage lust? Only in somebody's fantasy. What it simply means is that waves of people now called African Americans came to the New World from places in Africa that are physically and culturally very distinct, and each brought his or her heritage. All heritages have their tendencies, their acquired character, physicality, ways of seeing and hearing and doing things. That is what makes them heritages in the first place.

Clearly, there is in what we know as the black American heritage *something* that makes for a high proportion of people who play good ball. There is *something* — owing much to African musical tradition — that makes for the unprecedented rhythmic and harmonic interplay of jazz. And on and on. The mistake, though, is to infer from such broad matters of heritage that any individual black American will "naturally" display this or that tendency or talent. It doesn't work that way. Heritage is nutrition. People are creatures who feed. The results will always vary infinitely. And miraculously.

The only ironclad "natural" quality of being an African American is the human possibility to be anybody. Anybody at all. Many whites already know this. Others should learn it.

10. Blacks can safely be seen as "they."

No, "they" can't. If you are white, here is how to cure yourself of this mind-numbing habit: remind yourself that somewhere, at this very moment, a black person is summing up your entire identity with the word "they." How does it feel?

The Ten Worst Ideas Held by Black People about White People

1. White people want to be racist. They choose to be that way, even though they know better.

Q: How many racists does it take to install a lightbulb?
A: A hundred: one to screw in the bulb and ninety-nine to stare at it hatefully.

Okay, so racism is a not-too-bright response to American life. That is no excuse for blacks to tar-brush all whites who entertain racist notions as being bad people, or people who choose to harbor evil. Most whites are bombarded incessantly by racially skewed messages — news coverage, TV dramas, racial anxieties of friends and family — that turn black Americans into caricatures. One could argue that some whites, reared under such conditions of near brain-washing, never have a chance to believe otherwise.

It is temptingly easy for black people to demonize passively racist whites for embracing dumb ideas ("Blacks don't work hard enough"; "I'm nervous around them"). It is harder to recognize what is actually going on, which is that some whites simply believe what they are told, or fall back into lines of racial reasoning that they find comforting ("A white guy like me has no chance today").

When it comes to the camouflage-clad hate case who plays storm trooper in the woods on weekends, there is likely no room for civil consideration, even though one could argue that he himself is a casualty of racism. But when encountering most folk who entertain racist ideas, you have a choice as to how to react. Black people can curl up in a fetal position and turn their backs on racist white people (in effect encouraging them to be as prejudiced as they like). Or they can see the weakness of such people for what it is, declare it unacceptable, and stop at nothing to hold them, and society, accountable for it.

Yes, addressing racism among white friends and coworkers is aggravating. Sometimes it feels like a waste of time. Often there are politics to be considered. You make choices about what's worth talking about and what isn't. But just as whites should be willing to account for their hostility and resentment, so should you. If you're going to be angry at someone

about it, be willing to approach him or her about it.
And take it from there.

2. Only a white person can be racist.

Here's the argument: any black hatred toward whites
in America cannot be racism, because it is not based
on a history of officially sanctioned and organized
oppression. From an aerial view, there is a tidy truth
to this: wipe out the foul institutions that feed
racism — such as monopolies that increasingly de-
press wages — and the disease will disappear. But
here on the ground amid the slop, the illness is contagious. And the virus of hatred does not respect skin
color. When embittered black teenagers kick the crap
out of passersby because they can no longer stand the
sight of white people, and when a black passenger on
a bus makes a gesture of holding his nose in the presence of a white stranger, what do *you* call it? Use any
term you like: ethnic hate, revenge, reciprocal prejudice. Any way you look at it, it is surrendering to the
illness. And that will take black Americans nowhere.

3. In the end, a white person will always side with white people.

Ask three murdered white civil rights workers in Mississippi about that. Or any number of other whites who give the lie to such nonsense. If you are not willing to take any of the risks of engaging with people of other races, you might as well give up now.

4. Whites have it easy. They have nothing to complain about.

There is an understandable shortage of sympathy in the African-American community for the problems of American whites. For every white tale about suffering westbound homesteaders, there is a black story of horribly abused slaves who owned nothing. For every white complaint of muggings, there are black accounts of lynchings. For every white layoff, there are five jobs that never existed in African-American neighborhoods in the first place.

But this much should be obvious: that African Americans have suffered, arguably more than any other group in this country except for the American Indians, does not entitle us as blacks to ignore the suffering of others. If anything, it should enable us to understand others' suffering, and even to see how it might connect with our own. Whites who fear for their jobs, their health insurance, their safety, and their kids' public schools are not fantasizing these things. Even if their anxieties sometimes reflect exaggerated fears about black people, the underlying problems are real — for Americans of all colors. Treat them as such.

Tired of having white friends or coworkers deny your problems as an African American? Then do not deny theirs.

5. Why argue? A white person will never understand.

I know. It's a black thing. This is another way of saying, "I can't handle the wear and tear of dealing with white people who don't see my point of view as an African American. It's too hard. I give up."

It's a free country. Give up if you want to. But consider this: Who said there was ever going to be total understanding? Who said that the only acceptable outcome of any conversation was complete agreement? In a dialogue between a black person and a white one, maybe neither will ever fully understand what the other is trying to say. Maybe it's not about the pursuit of some holy grail of total understanding. Maybe it's about incremental understanding, about gaining ground in spite of friction. Maybe it's about not being afraid to argue, about not being afraid to not understand.

It seems to me that the real question, for any black person challenged to dialogue, is not, Why argue? but Why not?

6. All whites have an equal stake in racism.

It is a seductive fear: white people pressing in hatefully from every side, all with the same vested interest in preserving preferential treatment for themselves by discriminating against blacks. Forever. Like most seductive simplifications, it is misinformed. Racism does not have the same appeal and staying power for everyone. It will not last practically forever in every pantry, like canned peas. Racism's shelf life will vary, depending on whether particular whites have reason to question it. However ugly or virulent, it is not inherently indestructible.

For instance: some whites who live in isolated or high-walled communities might, like some antebellum slaveowners, see no reason to soften their hostility toward blacks unless forced to by civic upheaval or legislation. But many other whites, including some with whom you work or near whom you live, stand to gain quite a lot by ditching their prejudice sooner rather than later. The shared interests outweigh the racial divisions. When you declare such growth to be a flat-out impossibility for all whites, you invest racism with far more power than it possesses. And you render yourself blind to racism's weaknesses.

In fact, you begin to sound more and more like a racist yourself.

7. Whites have a permanent and unshakable monopoly on the American dream.

Here is one of the most catastrophic lies that black Americans have ever embraced. It plays itself out in a long list of beliefs, reinforced daily by a crushing lack of opportunity, that are especially destructive for African-American children: If you like to study and learn, you are acting white. If you learn to speak Standard English, you are an Uncle Tom. If you think that you have any chance for mainstream success, you are a chump.

The reality, of course, is that there is absolutely nothing in American culture that whites can claim belongs exclusively to them. Any and all of it can, and should, be explored and commandeered by blacks in any way we please. Paul Robeson's professors at Rutgers could not stop him from reading Marx. Trumpeter Wynton Marsalis reads Bach compositions with an understanding of those by Charlie Parker. Is he a compromised black man? For black Americans, getting one's teeth into the American midsection is not a matter of rights; it is a matter of access. And the idea that such territory is off-limits to blacks is both old and a dead end. It is what slaveowners commanded blacks to believe.

Even in its destructiveness, though, such abdication makes perfect sense to many African Americans. For them, the mainstream seems as remote and as inaccessible as any forbidden city. From the point of view of a community without jobs or decent schools, the mainstream does become a white man's land, and to declare it so becomes an act of defiance rather than submission.

Let's not be disingenuous: no solution short of political and economic change will bring the needed opportunities. But part of the answer also has to be a willingness to lay claim to what the mainstream has withheld instead of shunning it as a forever lost cause. Defiant surrender just isn't good enough.

8. Racism is white people's fault, so they should be the ones to address it.

Sure, and it was the shipbuilder's job to rescue people from the *Titanic*. Let the racists who cling to "unsinkable" white privilege go down with the ship. This water's cold. Learn to swim.

9. Whites are born ice people.

Black theories of abandoned albino infants in African forests notwithstanding, the time for intellectual Jell-O wrestling on questions of race has passed. Even white American criminologists quit measuring foreheads many decades ago, and Charles Murray, the *Bell Curve* cell-block captain, will be forgotten long before the first black American president is elected.

Black Americans know the power and potency of the African-American presence on these shores in all spheres — art, culture, learning, and public life. We also know that none of our endlessly varied talents and differences can be safely confined to anyone's rigid definition of the traits of "being black." So why would we try to force such silliness on whites? As revenge? As a fancied taste of their own racist medicine? Come on. To smile at one white person for wearing shorts in winter or another for losing the beat on the dance floor is one thing. To make dour pronouncements — as some blacks do smugly — of whites being genetically predisposed to chilly psychopathology is quite another.

Whether mean-spirited or just wrongheaded, such delusions are inexcusable. If you go for this claptrap, prepare for a visit from Charles Murray. He's coming over to measure your head.

10. Whites can safely be seen as "they."

No, "they" can't. If you are black, here is how to cure yourself of this mind-numbing habit: remind yourself that somewhere, at this very moment, a white person is summing up your entire identity with the word "they." How does it feel?

16

Nigger + Whitey:
Interracial Love and Racial Hate

black man and a white woman in a car stop at a traffic light. A white man pulls alongside in a pickup truck and locks his eyes on them. He stares at the two of them with such apoplectic rage that they almost expect his brain to burst, blood to spew out from behind his eyes. He grips the wheel and continues to stare, a skinny man of stone, eyes fixed on a white woman and black man through a long red light. What do they do? They make funny faces at him. They stick out their tongues, waggle their hands behind their ears, laugh. His face reddens. His expression says he might like to kill them, this nigger and Snow White in their sports car. But the light changes. Everyone drives away.

At a cocktail party hosted by friends, a West African woman introduces her white American husband to assorted guests of various nationalities and ethnicities. They all greet her husband warmly, with one obvious exception: the black Americans are cold to the point of rudeness. Later, the embarrassed host apologizes to the couple; some black Americans, the host tells them, seem to have a problem.

At a sidewalk café, a black man and white woman look up from their food to notice that their presence has attracted the furious attention of a table of three African-American women. The women have stopped eating, put down their forks, and are glowering. The very sight of a black man with a white woman has brought their pleasure to a momentarily screeching halt. Just as it has for the couple.

Interracial love in a nation racially at war. What could cut closer to the bone than our choice of those with whom we share flesh? Race is nothing: melanin, accident, physical scenery. Race is everything: slavery, self-love, self-hate. For interracial lovers, whether rich or poor, gay or straight, there is the same procession of scattered strangers who shout into your partnership their message that color counts. More than just public manners are abandoned. People are beaten up or killed for this, daughters and sons disowned, friends estranged, bitter recriminations flung:

"You'll date *anything* white," says a black woman to a black male friend after meeting his white girlfriend.

"You want that black lovin'," sneers a white man at his younger sister upon hearing that she has a date with a black man.

"You're ugly. They're better-looking," one black woman feels she is being told, without a word being spoken, when a black man dates a procession of white women.

"You're a loser. They're winners," one black man feels he is being told, with no words spoken, when a black woman dates a white man.

Let's not act surprised. With weapons stuffed in every nook and cranny of America's shared racial house, why should our bedroom be safe? Sex is the most potent expression of personal power we have. It is no accident that once upon a time in America, sweaty white men hacked off black penises and testicles while white women watched, or that today, young men on street corners still clutch their own family jewels. Still, the emotional abattoir that our country has made of interracial love and kisses nearly defies description. The legacy in broken hearts and bones —not to mention bruised feelings in restaurants — is more than we can know.

When I was a teenager, I was briefly sweet on a white girl I'll call Carol. She was smart and cute. She liked me, and I liked her. We went on a couple of dates, held hands, talked on the phone, felt warm inside. Then one day she wouldn't talk to me, wouldn't see me. Without explanation, it was over. I was as heartbroken as a teenager can manage to be. We both graduated without speaking of it again. But years later I saw Carol at a reunion, and I asked her why she had dumped me. She told me, through a tight throat, that she had been beaten by her grandfather and forbidden to ever see "that nigger" again.

I tell you this story not because there is anything special about it, but because there is not. It happens all the time. And it is about much more than whites simply "not liking" blacks, or vice versa. There is a nuclear-powered mythology that fuels our sexual racism, and it has blacks and whites bursting out of their skins to get at each other, sometimes with sex on their minds, sometimes with murder.

Why? Where does this lust/hate come from? And whether you are dating interracially or watching from the sidelines, how do you avoid becoming a casualty of society's passions?

Beneath It All

Let's start with what might be our deepest-running sexual neurosis: the age-old fascination with what goes on between black men and white women. The specter of marauding black men ravaging fair white women held spellbound by sexual magnetism is an

American article of faith. It was (and is) the obsession behind the compulsive lynching of black men — for which the alleged rape of white women has nearly always been offered as explanation. It is also the reason why so many movies and TV dramas about interracial romance portray simplistic, doomed trysts between virile black men and naive white women.

For example, *The Affair,* a 1995 made-for-cable movie, stars Courtney Vance as a dashing young black soldier stationed in England who tumbles into a torrid romance with the sheltered white wife of a passionless bureaucrat. They are discovered; she is coerced into claiming rape; he is hanged; she is forever heartbroken. The message — interracial love is irresistible poison — remains a common theme in novels and films, although hardly as pervasive today as in the days of such slavery bodice-rippers as *Mandingo.* Like the early American captivity narratives in which white women were abducted by Native Americans, this fable of black man/white woman relationships became cherished social text, despite countervailing evidence of healthy interracial love.

Why the erotic fairy tales? Because America's Puritan-influenced culture, preoccupied as it is with the bogeyman of sex, has eroticized the very idea of blackness by defining blacks as primitives. This served, early on, to justify slavery; the stereotype of black savagery was popularly embraced as the antithesis of the alleged dignity (and sexual restraint) of white life.

But gender mattered, too. As Cornel West has said in *Race Matters,* because ours is a sex-obsessed society in which men are expected to be the more sexually aggressive, the "primitive" stereotype heightened the sexual appeal of black men to whites, while demeaning the sexual appeal of black women (at least in public). The mantle of delicate and refined femininity fell instead to white women, in the form of a stereotype of white female sex appeal. To be sure, this "favored" sexual stature is no picnic for either black men or white women. Black men, as part of the bargain of being sexually glorified, remain the most reviled (and disproportionately imprisoned) men in America. And white women find themselves held to an impossible duality of goddess/whore femininity, while also facing the universal problems of sexual discrimination, abuse, and violence.

Still, it all sets the stage for today's hateful stares at black male/white female couples. The myth demeans everyone. Many black women, seeing this game for what it is (and seeing many black men play along), have grown bitterly resentful of having been left in the lurch. And many white men, simultaneously awed and threatened by the sexual hype about black men, seethe when they see "their" women "deserting" them for supposedly greener sexual pastures. Anger? Oh, yeah. And plenty of it.

Any African-American woman with dark skin, full lips, and kinky hair knows how it feels to have her beauty shunted aside in favor of the white version: light skin, straight hair, blue or green or gray eyes, and so on. Worse yet, black women have seen droves of African-American men buy into the notions that white women are prettier and that black men are more potent. It is as if legions of African-American men, over the centuries, have been willing to strike a nasty deal with white Americans: "I'll let you despise me if you'll sexually desire me." In the bargain, a great many black men *and* black women have come to accept the idea that the whiter-looking you are, the more attractive you are. Only a generation ago, it was common to hear black men boast to one another about having found a white woman, or a "high-yellow" (light-skinned) black woman. My mother remembers hearing black men of her generation, mocked for dating homely white women, snap back, "Well, at least she's white."

The attitude persists among some black American men today. One black female friend of mine, whenever she hears through the grapevine that some black man is dating a white woman, likes to ask, "Which is she, overweight or ugly?" The tendency, my friend insists — with some added topspin on her attitude — is for black men and less-attractive white women to "settle" for each other: he wants a white woman, she wants a man who will accept her. It is an image that provokes instant ire among many blacks, particularly women. When an interracial couple appears to fit this description, one can witness a trail of disdainful glances in their wake. As to how often this dynamic actually plays out within relationships, who can say? But it does happen. As does, under similar social pressures, the phenomenon of some black men "dating downward" in economic class in order to find white women who will accept them.

As if all of this were not enough, consider the terrible toll that poverty, prison, and drugs take on today's population of eligible African-American males. It is easy to understand the narrowing of options felt by many black women, particularly single and educated black women. For some, the mere sight of a black man with a white woman becomes, rightly or wrongly, a jabbing symbol of black men succumbing to the influence of white values. It hurts. This is where the glares, and the cutting of eyes, come from.

Certain white men also see red at the prospect of any turn-on between black men and white women, although such injury is pretty much limited to matters of ego. After all, white men still own more property, wield more political power, enjoy more social respect, and can date and marry among a broad range of women if they choose. To the extent that they are victims, it is from buying into the "jungle brute" stereotype of blacks, thereby dooming themselves to feeling like sexual wimps in comparison. Bet on it: when such a white man scowls at a black man and a white woman, his pain originates somewhere in the groin.

The same sexual-animal mythology can play out in how relationships between black women and white men are perceived. After all, whites applied the sex-hungry stereotype to black women as well, creating a "savage" fantasy parallel to that of black men. And this Puritan-based white caricature of the untamed black woman was accompanied by the desire to get naked with her. On the plantation, white men embraced one version of the feminine ideal in public, and another entirely in private — often by force. Rape was common and brutal. And the sexual dynamic between white master and female slave created its own world of supercharged symbolic roles: the white master as a figure who could bestow favor upon a sexually compliant black woman; the black man as a potential loser to the white man in the realm of being a "provider." With the diminished expectations by many black women (often heads of slave households) of the power of black men, and the emasculating sense of despair felt by many black men at their own perceived diminishment, the potential for relationships between black women and white men left a legacy of tension and mistrust.

And so a relationship between a black woman and a white man can evoke for some — and perhaps for themselves — stubborn historical stereotypes. Black men may sneer (though at great risk of hypocrisy) at the couple like spurned suitors, wondering to themselves what privilege the black woman is getting from her white mate. Maybe you remember, for example, the adjustment required of some black men in the 1980s when the media latched onto the story of upwardly mobile black women exercising their option to date white professional men. The angle played up in many of the stories — a sensational one, but fair — could be summed up as "What's good for the goose is good for the gander." In other words, if black men can date whites, so can black women. White women, for their part, may suck their teeth at white male/black female couples, as if in disdain of a white man's falling for what they assume to be the primal power and sexual abandon of a black woman. And blacks and whites alike may flinch at the very surprise of seeing, in public, an apparent rejection of cherished white female standards of beauty.

All of this, of course, goes deeper than gender or sexual preference. Whether straight, gay, lesbian, or bisexual, relationships involving black and white partners touch on nerves. They call up, inevitably, all manner of venerable stereotypes involving black men and black women and white women and white men. Insecurity, hypocrisy, prejudice, power: the whole conflagration trailing us, in the streets and bedrooms of America, like noisy shadows. How do lovers find peace in such a place?

Dealing with It

So you love someone who is white. Or someone who is black. And other people, crouched in various spots along your path, feel free to think their narrow-minded thoughts and fling their coded little accusations:

"You're a black stud on a white leash."

"You're a white woman who craves black meat."

"You're a black woman out for a white sugar daddy."

"You're an Uncle Tom who'll take anybody who's white."

"You're a black person with low self-esteem."

"You're a white person who's out to make a statement."

"You're desperate."

"You're pathetic."

All of which beg the question: Are you? Do you actually believe that white women are better-looking than black women? Do you presume to have no use for black men, and consider white men more attractive prospects? Do you seek, in black men or women, a bestial savagery your race lacks? These are fair questions. You ought to answer them. To yourself. To your satisfaction. Do you know who you are, where you come from, what heritage you own? Do you respect your own background and origins, and those of your partner? Do you find your lover's humanity to be more engaging than his skin color or his sexuality or her hair? Nobody can answer these questions but you. And, as an American raised on race like the rest of us, you had better answer them honestly if you expect anything close to inner peace in our color-obsessed society.

Look in the mirror. Look at how you treat your own ethnicity. Look at your patterns in choosing partners, if you can recognize any. Look at your partner's view of your ethnicity. See any changes that you need to make in yourself or your relationship? Make them. Feel any discomfort with who you are? Address it. Only when you have been willing to stare at yourself will you be able to hold on to your true identity in the face of others' spiteful stereotypes. Only when you have locked eyes with yourself will you become less vulnerable — on the street or at your parents' Thanksgiving dinner — to other people's harsh judgment of your choice of partners.

It is important, I think, for people who date interracially to understand the source of certain kinds of resentment without surrendering to it. The anger with which black women sometimes regard black male/white female relationships, for example, deserves to be taken seriously. This is no matter of petty jealousy. It is a naturally fierce reaction to the historical attack against black femininity — an attack in which some black men, to their collective discredit, have been accomplices by flocking to the Marilyn Monroe side of the theater in pursuit of white norms of femininity. The shame is not strictly one-sided; "white-is-right" values have also influenced black women, as in, for example, the popularity of alleged skin-lightening creams. The notion that kinky black hair *had* to be artificially straightened (as opposed to its being a matter of choice), and the labeling of naturally straight (Caucasian) hair as "good" hair, have reflected self-contempt among both black men and black women.

But the fact remains that while black women found themselves facing cosmetic rejection, some black men reinforced that very rejection through an explicit preference for white standards of beauty. For three-hundred-some–odd years. I'd call that a long insult. It would behoove you, if you are a black man, or if you are a white woman who loves a black man, to have some empathy for the resulting pain and anger on the part of African-American women. When black women give that stare, you should understand the source but reject the judgment. Respond, if you choose to, by looking back at them with a mixture of understanding and resolve. If, as a couple, you have built a relationship with respect for yourselves and your cultures, you have no explaining to do.

If you are a black woman with a white man, you don't owe black men any explanations, either, particularly given the history of black men in interracial romance. But you, too, can try to carry yourself with an understanding of the pain shared by black women and black men. The shared history of black American women and men has left deeply scraped spots on the souls of both. Neither is unscarred. In America's four-century interracial tryst, black women and black men have suffered the most harm. Both need to heal.

And what if you are someone on the outside glaring in, who disapproves of interracial relationships? Well, if you are able to reason, you need to know that your angry sizing up of interracial relationships is nowhere near as accurate as you think it is. Your own sensitivities get in your way. You scrutinize couples for the glaring signs — educated black person dating down, white person out for dark thrills, black person who has given up on dating blacks — and you think you find them. But the truth is that much of the time, you cannot even begin to tell by looking. There is simply too much that you do not know, too much anger and too little information. And if you do happen to correctly diagnose one couple's dysfunction on a street corner, is it worth having flung unjustified fury in the faces of so many others? I can't see how.

Even if you are acquainted with a person and disapprove of his or her black or white partner, your opinion is still worth no more than the experience it is etched on. But when you make snap judgments of people in public, based solely on the film loops in your own mind, you commit a worse offense: you are dumping your garbage into the personal space of perfect strangers.

I know: if you are an African-American woman, in particular, it might be hard not to feel your jaw tighten when you see a black man hand in hand with a white woman. You know the damage done by the widely held black stud/white princess fantasy; the decades of racial indoctrination; the skin-bleaching creams and corrosive hair-straightening compounds and hot combs; the little black girls who drape shirts from their heads, tossing the fabric in imitation of long, straight hair; the black men who lose their minds to the Hollywood blond factory.

But think about this: if you happened to meet a white man, and felt attracted to him, and proceeded to build, to your mutual delight, a loving relationship based upon personal and cultural respect and compatibility, how would you then feel if utter strangers sucked their teeth at the two of you? And made you objects of public scorn at random intervals?

Some black men and white women may date for the wrong reasons. And some date for the right ones. People of every color and nationality date for right and wrong reasons, or combinations of the two. It seems to me that those couples who have managed to swim above racist stereotype do not deserve your glares. They deserve your respect. And on a street corner or in a restaurant, you cannot tell which interracial couple is which.

Wouldn't it be better to be angry, if at all, at situations about which you knew the details, and in which you could accomplish something through two-way communication? If your brother or sister or close friend continually dates in a way that appears to use race destructively — as a way to get at the family or seek exotic thrills or compensate for insecurities — then maybe the two of you can talk. Maybe. But barring any such personal entanglements, your aiming corrective commentary — verbal or nonverbal — at interracial couples is way out of line.

If, on the other hand, you are a black or white American who is simply dead set against any interracial touching of the skin, what can I tell you? Take a deep breath. African Americans are not shipping out, and neither are whites, and the longer we share a nation, the more of us will try dinner and a movie together. It is miraculous, in its way, that in spite of centuries of slogging through stereotypes, happy black/white couples happen at all. They are a triumph over a history of war. The interracial couple at the next table, about whom you are prepared to whisper unkindly, may have a more fulfilling relationship than you and your own mate.

Early in our history, America turned interracial love — the simple act of love between people of different colors and heritages — into Interracial Love, an epic of lust, slaughter, cultural betrayal, and reconciliation. It is time now for us to reclaim lowercase interracial love, real-life love as it happens between black and white people who want to eat and to dance, who want to help build neighborhoods, who want to raise children who will carry our cultures forward together. It is a job as messy and as thankless as any in the world. Victory — the last stare endured, the last family harassed, the last heart broken — will be known only by the absence of trials we now suffer. None of which, I imagine, will be missed.

It is time that we lost the assumptions, the blind accusations, the unseeing glares, and found instead the human capacity not to constantly seek out the worst in one another.

Maybe, just maybe, we will see fit to spare ourselves.

Epilogue

Race Manners

Not long ago, on one of the many radio programs that I listen to faithfully, I heard an international affairs expert from Africa explain in wrenching detail the increasing worldwide use of child soldiers in warfare. In violation of international standards, he said, many countries are putting more and more eight- and ten-year-olds on the front lines, where they frequently commit gruesome atrocities. He gave many reasons: shortages of adults; the availability of orphans, many of them desperate for food and protection; the malleability of child trainees.

Then he paused. There was also an underlying reason, he said: the breakdown, in the devastation of war, of a culture's social contract with children. He used a word in his native language that translated roughly as the "cleanliness" of a warrior's moral claim. Traditionally in his culture, he said, combatants who abused children or broke other social contracts were viewed as having soiled this claim. But today the pact — what we might call the "manners" of warfare — is shattered. Children are attacking villages. And dying in droves.

Americans might — on our own scale of catastrophe — say something similar, of not only our treatment of our children but our treatment of ourselves. For lack of manners — for lack of social contracts — we endure unfairness and mistrust and rage, ducking and running, as in wartime, to save our own skins. And, with our hostilities over race at a rolling boil, some of us soil our own claims.

We need to explore racial manners because the alternative is to dodge racial shrapnel. I mean "racial manners" not in the punishing sense of a ruler slap on the knuckles, but in the collaborative sense of manners as consideration reached through interchange. Not by political decree. Not by authority of anyone's gospel. But by venturing to say what we think to one another while still being willing to consider changing our minds. And by pooling what we agree upon as we go. This book is my offering of how we might start that everyday process. What I have written is what I believe. On some things, I may at some point change my mind. But on any of this, you might argue with me, shake your head, see it your own way. Which leads to the real questions: What do *you* think? What would *you* do? What should *you* say?

These are exactly the questions on race that Americans need to begin to answer. We need to be willing to take these matters on, to turn and face each other in elevators, to expose fears and wounded feelings over coffee, to argue, pose dilemmas, trade answers, confront obstinacy, demand to be heard. Yes, some people are too far gone for this process, too lost in the trenches. But most are not. All that we need in order to start talking is for one of us — any of us — to speak up.

To paraphrase Judith Martin (otherwise known as Miss Manners), the purpose of manners is to help people to be as comfortable as possible in one another's company. If we will invest in manners for the sake of an enjoyable dinner, surely we will do so for the sake of our survival.

See you at the table.